The New York Times

LOOKING FORWARD

Online Gaming

THE SURGE OF ESPORTS AND MOBILE GAMING

THE NEW YORK TIMES EDITORIAL STAFF

Published in 2019 by New York Times Educational Publishing
in association with The Rosen Publishing Group, Inc.
29 East 21st Street, New York, NY 10010

First Edition

The New York Times
Alex Ward: Editorial Director, Book Development
Phyllis Collazo: Photo Rights/Permissions Editor
Heidi Giovine: Administrative Manager

Rosen Publishing
Megan Kellerman: Managing Editor
Michael Hessel-Mial: Editor
Greg Tucker: Creative Director
Brian Garvey: Art Director

Cataloging-in-Publication Data
Names: New York Times Company.
Title: Online gaming: the surge of esports and mobile gaming /
edited by the New York Times editorial staff.
Description: New York : New York Times Educational Publishing,
2019. | Series: Looking forward | Includes glossary and index.
Identifiers: ISBN 9781642821345 (library bound) | ISBN
9781642821338 (pbk.) | ISBN 9781642821352 (ebook)
Subjects: LCSH: Internet games—Juvenile literature. | Computer
games—Juvenile literature. | Mobile games—Juvenile literature.
Classification: LCC GV1469.15 O555 2019 | DDC 794.8—dc23

Manufactured in the United States of America

On the cover: In addition to esports competitions and the
evolution of mobile games, online gaming has also expanded
across sites such as YouTube and Twitch, facilitating a more
diverse array of gaming communities than ever before; Schedivy
Pictures Inc./DigitalVision/Getty Images.

Contents

7   Introduction

CHAPTER 1

Massively Multiplayer Online Gaming

10   Go to the Mattresses (No, It's Not a Mob War) BY STEVEN ZEITCHIK

16   Even in a Virtual World, 'Stuff' Matters BY SHIRA BOSS

24   It's Love at First Kill BY STEPHANIE ROSENBLOOM

30   Four Hours of Screen Time? No Problem BY DIANE MEHTA

33   Disruptions: Minecraft, an Obsession and an Educational Tool
     BY NICK BILTON

36   Behind League of Legends, E-Sports's Main Attraction
     BY DAVID SEGAL

47   The Minecraft Generation BY CLIVE THOMPSON

66   Closing the Gender Gap, One E-Battle at a Time BY HAYLEY KRISCHER

69   A New Phase for World of Warcraft's Lead Designer: His Own
     Start-Up BY NICK WINGFIELD

72   A Non-Gamer's Guide to Fortnite, the Game That Conquered All
     the Screens BY SANDRA E. GARCIA

CHAPTER 2

The Fast-Paced Market for Mobile Games

75 Will Zynga Become the Google of Games? BY MIGUEL HELFT

83 From the Land of Angry Birds, a Mobile Game Maker Lifts Off
BY NICK WINGFIELD

85 Candy Crush and the Curve of Impressiveness BY DANIEL VICTOR

87 Executive at Struggling Rovio, Maker of Angry Birds, Pushes
Silver Lining BY MARK SCOTT

89 Bobby Kotick's Activision Blizzard to Buy King Digital, Maker of
Candy Crush BY MICHAEL J. DE LA MERCED AND NICK WINGFIELD

93 Pokémon Go See the World in Its Splendor BY AMY BUTCHER

98 Mario, Nintendo's Mustachioed Gaming Legend, Arrives
on iPhones BY NICK WINGFIELD AND VINDU GOEL

102 How I Became Addicted to Online Word Games BY LIESL SCHILLINGER

107 An Angry Birds Empire: Games, Toys, Movies and Now an I.P.O.
BY CHAD BRAY

111 China Embraces a Game About a Traveling Frog BY KAROLINE KAN
AND AUSTIN RAMZY

CHAPTER 3

Esports and Gaming as Public Spectacle

113 The Land of the Video Geek BY SETH SCHIESEL

121 Video Gaming on the Pro Tour, for Glory but Little Gold
BY RICHARD NIEVA

126 Seeking to Be Both N.F.L. and ESPN of Video Gaming
BY ALAN FEUER

134 What's Twitch? Gamers Know, and Amazon Is Spending
$1 Billion on It BY NICK WINGFIELD

138 Activision Buys Major League Gaming to Broaden Role
in E-Sports BY NICK WINGFIELD

141 Esports Sees Profit in Attracting Female Gamers
BY GREGORY SCHMIDT

146 Big Ten Universities Entering a New Realm: E-Sports
BY MARC TRACY

148 Gamer's Death Pushes Risks of Live Streaming Into View
BY DANIEL E. SLOTNIK

152 All We Want to Do Is Watch Each Other Play Video Games
BY NELLIE BOWLES

160 With Twitch, Amazon Tightens Grip on Live Streams of
Video Games BY JOHN HERRMAN

CHAPTER 4

Struggles in Gaming Communities

165 Feminist Critics of Video Games Facing Threats in 'GamerGate'
Campaign BY NICK WINGFIELD

170 It's Game Over for 'Gamers' BY ANITA SARKEESIAN

173 Twine, the Video-Game Technology for All BY LAURA HUDSON

185 In the Documentary 'GTFO,' Female Video Gamers Fight Back
BY ROBERT ITO

189 How Gaming Helped Launch the Attack of the Internet Trolls
   BY QUENTIN HARDY

193 Why Some Men Don't Work: Video Games Have Gotten
   Really Good BY QUOCTRUNG BUI

196 The Real Problem With Video Games BY SETH SCHIESEL

199 Video Game Addiction Tries to Move From Basement to
   Doctor's Office BY TIFFANY HSU

206 Endless Gaming May Be a Bad Habit. That Doesn't Make It a
   Mental Illness. BY BENEDICT CAREY

210 Glossary
212 Media Literacy Terms
215 Media Literacy Questions
217 Citations
221 Index

Introduction

EVEN THE SIMPLEST video games are characterized by the craft that goes into building a virtual world we enter. Whether we're directing abstract blocks on a grid, hunting for a red potion to restore our dwindling health or waving a plastic wand to direct Wario's tennis backhand on a screen, we are playing by rules that a game designer has created for us to play. By pressing start, we accept those rules.

However, gaming is defined not just by these rules, but by what we bring to them. We discover moves the designer didn't anticipate. We create communities of players, turning in-game terminology into slang. Players become e-athletes, and dynamic personalities become streaming stars. Communities turn games into franchises and gaming into culture. As the internet has evolved, these features of gaming have accelerated, especially in massively multiplayer online games and mobile gaming.

Massively multiplayer online (MMO) gaming began in the 1990s with platforms such as EverQuest, but when Blizzard Entertainment, the studio behind the popular game Warcraft, developed its online World of Warcraft in 2004, MMOs became a firm part of the cultural landscape. The most popular games were often fantasy or science fiction battle frenzies, but others embraced a quieter side. Second Life allowed people to build fashionable avatars in slick digital spaces, while Minecraft offered a quiet space to build and learn. And as games have evolved, breakouts such as League of Legends and Fortnite have taken center stage in the big business of gaming.

Cultures of video gaming grow, and with them grow the culture of watching them. As YouTube and Twitch have allowed us to watch others play, a once solitary activity has become a new form of popular media. We don't simply watch the playing; we watch the commentary,

Esports team Samsung White during the quarterfinal round of the 2014 League of Legends World Championships.

the in-jokes and plugs for upcoming games that give significance to our own playing. But the play is never quite lost, as competitive gaming begins to command viewership on par with mainstream sports. While South Korea was an early leader in the pop culture of competitive esports, American promoters have worked to make video game championships as exciting as traditional sporting events.

While MMO game development tends to have budgets rivaling Hollywood, another approach to game development has emerged: games delivered via mobile app. Based on novelty and simple gameplay, mobile gaming has been responsible for expanding the gaming market to casual players. The industry is noticing. Rovio, the maker of Angry Birds, now earns millions on the strength of its brand alone, and Candy Crush developer King Digital was purchased by Blizzard Activision in an attempt to corner the mobile market. Nintendo, notoriously cautious in its business model, enjoyed a stunning coup with its mobile game Pokémon Go. Though mobile games don't appeal to the "traditional" market, they show how our definition of games continues to evolve.

Building on the connectivity and commercial potential of the internet, online gaming has become one of our primary modes of entertainment, a means of making friends, expressing ourselves and building skills. However, these new tools have led to unexpected personal and social consequences, in the form of community conflicts and unhealthy relationships with gaming. Social critics have observed the predominantly male gamer demographic and the efforts of some gaming communities to exclude women from participation. The short-lived GamerGate campaign, during which many women were harassed and threatened in the name of "ethics in gaming journalism," suggested that gaming culture had inadvertently become a hostile, closed environment. Many began discussions of newer, better ways to think about gaming in our lives, representing broader points of view and discouraging the trolling that often accompanies online gamer culture. And many others investigated gaming itself for encouraging gaming addiction. Is it possible to become addicted to playing video games? Is it a mental illness? Who is responsible, the game designer or the player? Now that gaming is fully mainstream, these hard questions about the effects — both social and personal — of video games are building in urgency.

The struggles of online gaming should, in the end, remind us of the role we play in video game culture. Though every click is brought to us by a multimillion dollar budget, plus hours of labor by developers and executives, video games are the active expression of our own creative energies, our own imaginations and aspirations. Our interactions transform the games we play. The obsessive drive of the Twitch streamer, esports champion or even the relentless Words With Friends player in our friend group, is awakened in us and given shape by the games that define our lives.

CHAPTER 1

Massively Multiplayer Online Gaming

Massively multiplayer online gaming began in the 1990s, and by the mid 2000s, it had emerged as a cultural force. People's virtual lives in these interactive games became a new way of expressing themselves and building relationships. These resulted in new languages and even, occasionally, marriages. As young people grew up with these games, developing skills outside of the traditional classroom, some began evaluating games as educational tools. As the 2000s gave way to the 2010s, some games became so prevalent that even the non-gaming world took notice: Fortnite was the most popular game of 2018.

Go to the Mattresses (No, It's Not a Mob War)

BY STEVEN ZEITCHIK | JULY 10, 2005

BUTLER, N.J. — At least once a month, James Callari, 36, grabs some cans of Red Bull, packs up his computer and tells his girlfriend he is going out to play some video games. Don't bother waiting up, he'll say — he won't be back for two or three days.

Mr. Callari's destination is a LAN party, an intense, almost ritualistic convocation of gamers that has been springing up — almost invisibly — in pockets all over New Jersey.

In hotel conference rooms, firehouses, paramedic call centers — anywhere that offers enough cheap real estate (and electric power) — men are quietly gathering for gaming benders that by turns resemble an epic paintball match, a scene from the movie "Fight Club," a high-tech game of "Dungeons and Dragons" and an Iron John meeting.

Video arcades usually allow only one or two people to play a game at one time — bad news for modern gamers, who like to play in groups.

But through high-powered temporary servers, local area networks, or LANs, enable computers in a concentrated area to communicate. For Mr. Callari and his cohorts, LANs are the ticket to video-game orgies, sessions of intense play and bonding that can last days. Seventy-two hours is not unheard of. Computer equipment is obligatory. Air mattresses are optional.

"Once you get that sense of camaraderie, you never want to leave," said Mr. Callari, who lives in Summit.

Long past midnight on a recent Saturday, a dozen boys and men between the ages of 10 and 40 sat squinting in front of terminals. They were at a volunteer firehouse they had rented in Butler, on a quiet street next to a cemetery. Behind a room filled with hoses, award plaques and a gleaming fire truck sat the paraphernalia of the LAN life — rows of snazzy C.P.U.'s, oversize monitors and mounds of snaking wires. A U.F.O. landing would not have seemed much stranger.

The party's organizer was the boyishly gregarious John Pezzino. Outside the LAN matrix, Mr. Pezzino lives in Butler and works a desk job at U.P.S. In it, he is known as Murdock, and he calls the shots. "UT?" he says, the abbreviation for the game Unreal Tournament. Then, in reference to which mode they would play, "Capture the Flag? Let's jump on."

With that, teammates erupt with warnings; opponents intimidate with (usually) good-natured digs; neighbors whisper conspiratorially. On the screen, perfect digital representations of masked men toting weaponry leap from rooftops and run across deserts. Gamers mechanically swig designer caffeine drinks with names like Bawls, their eyes sweating with the possibility of a virtual escape, their mouths motoring off instructions.

If the office IT guys ever threw a rave, it would probably look something like this.

"Warlord, where are you? Get out of there."

"I'm almost out of health."

"Dad, did you like the way I killed you?"

"My health's, like, really gone."

"Spray and prey, spray and prey. Beautiful."

"Well, I'm dead."

Of course, LAN parties are not limited to New Jersey. California is a hotbed, and the Dallas mega-LAN Quakecon draws thousands. But the Garden State is fast becoming its Northeast capital. One of the country's biggest LANs, the GXL — a three-day, 500-person bacchanal — takes place at a rescue squad in Millville. And then there are the smaller gatherings nearly every week, run by at least five separate groups.

"Jersey has things other places don't — a lot of space and a lot of gamers," says a LAN-er who goes by the tag Kobalt and runs Weekend Wars, a South Jersey LAN. (In his non-LAN life, Kobalt is Mike Kowarski, who describes his career as "on the law-enforcement side of things.")

Many of the games LAN-ers play are first-person shooters. To those of us for whom Frogger still represents the cutting edge, this can be a tricky concept. It basically means that no gamer can see the whole game at once, instead viewing it strictly from the perspective of their own character.

Paradoxically, this enhances the thrill; you're never quite able to trust your eyes. It also increases the team factor. A nearby gamer either has your back — or is waiting to put a bullet in it.

Games also last a lot longer than they used to. The abundant number of virtual layouts, or maps, leads to complicated expeditions.

But if the goals of particular games vary, what doesn't change is the stakes: Team pride and individual skills, measured by rankings of things like "kills" and "health," which the computer periodically spits out.

As a result, LAN-ers hone their craft with the diligence of a trained actor; for all the yelling, a LAN party can sometimes seem more like a play rehearsal, complete with furrowed brows and shared advice.

As with many subcultures, language can be an unresolved thicket ("You got to get kills, and then you can kill").

As the night wears on, though, more recognizable forms of conversation flower. Men ogle one another's computer equipment. Some segue from Quake and Doom to life and love.

In one corner of the room on Saturday, Mr. Callari is ruminating on the vagaries of relationships.

"Inviting a woman to a LAN party is like inviting your wife to meet your mistress," he says to a group of five who have gathered around his chair. "It's not that you can't do it, but why would you?"

Mr. Callari, who goes by the tag Tora Bora Kid, is an unofficial leader in the LAN hierarchy. An electrician with an absurdist streak, he dresses in what you might call Haute Matrix — black dress shirt embossed with a black flower, black dress slacks and black aviator sunglasses (at midnight).

When asked if LAN parties ever ruined any of his relationships, he replies, "Yes," with a slight hint of pride.

Given how much LAN can feel like a religion, it is no surprise that each party plays off the same creation myth. It goes something like this:

One or two friends sit home, playing games online. But they're tired of being separated from teammates. So they invite some people to bring over their computers. Before long, the gathering becomes too big. (Mr. Pezzino's moment of revelation came when he had to take apart his bed to accommodate gamers at his Waldwick apartment.) So they seek out a new place. Word-of-mouth grows. A LAN party is born.

What is striking about LAN parties is how much they counter the notion of the video game as an isolating force. Across New Jersey's suburbs and towns, it is not lone figures in dark basements, but groups of 10 or 20 sharing an uncanny, if square, kinship.

"Anyone can play a game online," Mr. Kowarski says. "But it's not the same as being able to yell at them across the room."

While not technically a secret — most parties welcome new members — the gatherings thrive underground. Locations are revealed only shortly before each event. Word spreads via the scene or through cryptic postings on sites with gangsta-geek names like s2i.org, for shoot2ill.

Turf wars are common to LAN scenes, and New Jersey is especially tangled. The s2i guys don't like the GXL guys. NJLanParty has been ripped off by NewJerseyLan, according to Weekend Wars. (NewJersey-Lan has since gone silent.) LAN cafes — cyber cafes that provide LAN gaming — are to be scoffed at, though Mr. Kowarski allows they are not all bad because "they could be a gateway drug" for LAN parties.

And many LAN-ers hate Counterstrikers, the fiends who exclusively play a popular older shooter called Counterstrike.

"They cheat," Mr. Callari says. "And they're so competitive."

LAN parties have come a long way since their basement days. Sensing an obsessive audience, sponsors like Red Bull and the graphics firm Nvidia have begun to get involved. Some parties are also now infiltrated by "traders" — people who want to exploit the speedy network to share movie and music files. Prizes and betting can run to the hundreds of dollars.

Yet the scene retains a purity; it's more skater park than X Games. Few organizers make a profit, and gamers pay just a small fee to cover costs.

"Most of us just want to play," says Gregg McCarthy of Old Bridge, who runs the site NJGamers.

LAN parties also look to initiate new members, and many fathers will bring sons. At the Butler LAN, Mr. Callari explained to Ryan Price, a 10-year-old up way past his bedtime, how gaming used to be.

"We didn't have hard drives," he said. "We had to put everything on a floppy disk."

The boy nodded, but the befuddled look on his face said, "What's a floppy disk?"

And like most subcultures, the underground does not always translate above ground. Those who rent out the space to LAN-ers have, perhaps understandably, reservations upon seeing dozens of sleep-deprived souls showing up with large suitcases of equipment as though at a high-tech vampire convention. (Perhaps as a result, many LAN parties now donate profits to local causes.) Not to mention all the spouses shaking their head as the males prepare for what seem like a very odd hunting trip.

Somewhere around 1 a.m. in Butler, as people mill about between games, Mr. Pezzino tells how the fire captain who had rented him the hall hassled him when he saw the equipment they were dragging in.

"I just want to go somewhere where we're appreciated, you know?" Mr. Pezzino says. A few others nod, and Lou, a LAN-er with slick blond hair and a pile of software guides, says, "Well, that's not going to happen," in a you-should-know-better tone.

Mr. Pezzino pauses as he uploads a version of the next game. Then, looking contemplative, he says, "Yeah, I guess that's true."

Even in a Virtual World, 'Stuff' Matters

BY SHIRA BOSS | SEPT. 9, 2007

IT'S PAYDAY FOR Janine Hawkins. Not in the real world, where she is a student at Nipissing University in Ontario, but in the online world of Second Life, where she is managing editor of the fashion magazine Second Style.

Ms. Hawkins, who in Second Life takes on the persona of Iris Ophelia, a beauty with flowing hair and flawless skin, keeps a list of things she wants to buy: the latest outfits from the virtual fashion mecca Last Call, a new hairstyle from a Japanese designer, slouchy boots. When she receives her monthly salary in Linden dollars, the currency of Second Life, she spends up to four hours shopping, clicking and buying. After a year and a half, she owns 31,540 items.

Living it up in Second Life is a break from Ms. Hawkins's part-time job as a French translator, but she works just as hard in the virtual world.

Last month, she earned 40,000 Linden dollars ($150), for interviewing designers, arranging fashion shoots and writing about trends in Second Life, called SL by frequent users. "I usually spend what I earn," Ms. Hawkins said. "It's entertaining."

It also says a lot about the real world, especially when it comes to earning and spending money.

When people are given the opportunity to create a fantasy world, they can and do defy the laws of gravity (you can fly in Second Life), but not of economics or human nature. Players in this digital, global game don't have to work, but many do. They don't need to change clothes, fix their hair, or buy and furnish a home, but many do. They don't need to have drinks in their hands at the virtual bar, but they buy cocktails anyway, just to look right, to feel comfortable.

Second Life residents find ways to make money so they can spend it to do things, look impressive, and get more stuff, even if it's made only of pixels. In a place where people should never have to clean out their closets, some end up devoting hours to organizing their things, purging, even holding yard sales.

"Why can't we break away from a consumerist, appearance-oriented culture?" said Nick Yee, who has studied the sociology of virtual worlds and recently received a doctorate in communication from Stanford. "What does Second Life say about us, that we trade our consumerist-oriented culture for one that's even worse?"

Second Life, a three-dimensional world built by hundreds of thousands of users over the Internet, is also being used for education, meetings, marketing and more obvious game playing. It's a wide world with a lot going on, in multiple languages, and it can be real-life enhancing for populations who are isolated for physical, mental, or geographic reasons. But as a petri dish for examining what makes many of us tick, Second Life reveals just how deep-seated the drive is to fit in, look good and get ahead in a material world.

Janine Hawkins with her Second Life avatar Iris Ophelia. In the virtual world, Ms. Hawkins earns Linden dollars and spends them freely.

Many residents have lived the American dream in Second Life, and built Linden-dollar fortunes through entrepreneurship. In what could have been an ideal world, however, or one where anyone could be a Harry Potter, Second Life has an up-and-down economy, mortgage payments, risky investments, land barons, evictions, designer rip-offs, scams and squatters. Not to mention peer pressure.

"Second Life is about getting the better clothes and the bigger build and the reputation as a better builder," said Julian Dibbell, author of "Play Money," which chronicles his year of trying to make a living by trading virtual goods in online games. "The basic activity is still the keeping up with the Joneses, or getting ahead of the Joneses, rat race game."

To have a Second Life, one needs a computer, the Second Life software, and a high-speed Internet connection. You use a credit card to buy Lindens, and Lindens earned during the game can be converted back into dollars via online currency exchanges. Players start by choosing one of the standard characters, called an avatar, and can roam the world by flying or "teleporting" (click and go). Nobody can go hungry, there is no actual need for warmer clothes or shelter, and there is much to do without buying Lindens.

But walking around in a standard avatar, when there are so many ways to buy a better appearance, is like showing up for the first day of school dressed differently than all the other kids. You stick out as different, as an SL "newbie."

"It's hard not to fall into that," Mr. Yee said. "There are shops everywhere, so it's easy to say, 'Oh, O.K., I guess I'll get a better pair of jeans.' "

Second Life was started in 2003 by a Silicon Valley techie inspired by a sci-fi novel, "Snow Crash." It is owned by a private company called Linden Lab. The original idea of the game was to unleash creativity. Residents don't have to wear the latest fashions; they don't have to look — or act — human at all. They can take any animal, robotic, or inanimate form they want.

And while there is a minority population of animal characters, and wearing butterfly wings is currently in vogue for humans, for the most part the population is young women bursting from their blouses and young men bulging with muscle. (Underneath the clothes are cyber genitalia, sold separately. Mark Wallace, a blogger who writes about Second Life, explained that the parts are not fashion accessories but rather "a functional appliance" for, ahem, entertainment purposes.)

While a frequent criticism of Second Life is that spaces are often empty and that there's "nothing to do," a crowd can be found at the mall, just as it can in suburbia. For example, the Xcite! store, which sells body parts, is "always crawling with avatars," said Mr. Wallace, co-author of a forthcoming book, "The Second Life Herald." Fashion is big business in Second Life, along with entertainment and land development.

Big corporations like Toyota have set up islands in Second Life for marketing. Calvin Klein came up with a virtual perfume. Kraft set up a grocery store featuring its new products. But those destinations are not popular.

"These brands that have this real-world cachet are meaningless in Second Life, so most are ignored," said Wagner James Au, who blogs and writes books about Second Life. "Just showing up and announcing 'We're Calvin Klein' isn't going to get you anywhere." American Apparel closed its virtual clothing shop, and Wells Fargo abandoned the island it had set up to teach about personal finance.

Second Life exclusives do exist: A magic wand was a hot item at one point, and the sex bed is currently in demand. ("If you lie on it with more than one avatar, it's like you're in a porn movie," Mr. Au explained.)

But the more mundane items are what really drive the economy: clothes, gadgetry, night life, real estate. "People buy these huge McMansions in Second Life that are just as ugly as any McMansions in real life, because to them that is what's status-y," Mr. Wallace said. "It's not as easy as we think to let our imaginations run wild, in Second Life or in real life."

Mitch Ratcliffe, an entrepreneur and blogger, was an early resident of Second Life and built a house with a lake. But he was soon disillusioned with the upkeep involved with owning the property. "I don't see why I would want my second life to be about the same striving and profit that my first is," Mr. Ratcliffe wrote in a blog entry about his Second Life adventures. He eventually reincarnated himself as Homeless Hermes.

"People come by, see the user name and tell me how sorry they are that I don't have a home. Why?" he wrote. "It's very middle class, very staid in the way economic stigma is attached to a failure to get to work." In the meantime, Homeless Hermes took up buying and selling virtual land and has pocketed the equivalent of $800.

Land is the biggest-ticket item in Second Life, with Linden Lab selling islands for $1,675, plus a $295-a-month maintenance charge.) Catherine A. Fitzpatrick, a Russian translator in New York who in Second Life is a landlord known as Prokofy Neva, got into the game three years ago and now owns hundreds of apartment buildings, houses and stores that she rents out to about 1,500 tenants who pay from $1.50 a month to $150 a month. She takes several hundred dollars a month out of the game to pay real-world bills. Prokofy Neva herself does not have a house. "If I did, I would rent it out," she said. "Why not make money from it?"

She has, however, turned over virtual acreage for a land preserve and public use. She and an architect friend were initially entranced by the idea of creating artistic homes that could defy gravity, but they discovered that there wasn't demand for that in Second Life.

"The average person wants a ranch house or a beach house," she said. "They don't want even Frank Lloyd Wright." (She added, "These people are my customers, so I respect that.")

Some residents do wear grunge clothing — itself a status symbol in Second Life because of the difficulty of replicating ripped and stained clothing digitally. But the largest slice of the population follows the crowd, and the crowd is not dressing up as dragons.

"The money is in the real-looking stuff: making skins with red lips and smoky eyes, and stiletto boots," said Ms. Hawkins, the Second Life fashion writer. First comes something popular, then the knockoffs. Soon everyone has one. "People go for similar looks and similar things," she said.

In Ms. Hawkins's online closet are avatars that let her move around as a rubber ducky or as a fruit salad encased in gelatin. But those identities are novelty items that usually stay on the shelf. When she goes out in virtual public, Ms. Hawkins usually takes the form of Ms. Ophelia, who has more than 250 pairs of shoes.

Items are real-world cheap — an outfit usually costs $2 to $5 — but they can add up quickly. "It's so easy to buy something, you don't realize how much you're spending," said Carrie Mandel, a homemaker and mother in Chicago who spends two work days a week as well as evenings and weekends on her Second Life business, selling pets.

One coveted status symbol in Second Life is a souped-up muscle car called the Dominus Shadow. It currently costs 2,368 Linden dollars, about $9 at the current rate of 268 Linden per dollar. Many players pay that much every month for premium membership that lets them own land, and all are sitting at computers with high-speed Internet access. So why don't more people treat themselves to the prized possession of a Dominus?

"It's expensive in-world," said Daniel Terdiman, author of the forthcoming book "Entrepreneur's Guide to Second Life." "You don't think of how much things cost in real dollars; you think in Linden dollars. When something is expensive, even though it comes out to a few dollars, a lot of people don't want to spend that much money."

Although Linden dollars can be bought with a credit card, there is evidence that the in-world economy is self-sustaining, with many players compelled to earn a living in-world and live on a budget.

Surprisingly, many take on low-paying jobs. They work as nightclub bouncers, hostesses, sales clerks and exotic dancers for typical wages of 50 to 150 Linden dollars an hour, the equivalent of 19 to 56 cents. A recent classified ad stated: "I am looking for a good job in SL. I am sick of working off just tips." This job seeker listed potential occupations as landscaper, personal assistant, actor, waitress and talent scout.

Second Life players are evidently discovering what inheritors have struggled with for generations: It's not as much fun to spend money you haven't earned. Apparently, despite the common lottery-winning fantasies, all play and no work is a dull game, after all.

"People don't take jobs just for the money," said Dan Siciliano, who teaches finance at Stanford Law School and has studied the economies of virtual worlds. "They do it to feel important and be rewarded."

And to buy more things. "A lot of exotic dancers want to become models, so they can earn more money to buy more clothes," Ms. Hawkins said.

It's not just vanity that drives people to dress up in Second Life. It's also seen as good for business. Ms. Fitzpatrick, the landlady, says she doesn't really care about how her avatar looks. But she cares about what prospective tenants think. "I felt I had to go, finally, and buy the hair and the suit," she said, "or my customers might think I'm too weird."

Appearances count in Second Life's financial world, too. Banks and stock exchanges are housed in huge, formal structures draped in marble and glass. "People in the banking industry wear shiny silver suits and are absurdly tall and have hired a couple people to walk behind them in black suits with earbuds and shoulder holsters," said Benjamin Duranske, a lawyer who blogs about legal issues related to the virtual world.

The stock exchanges and banks in SL are imposing, but they are unregulated and unmonitored. Investors fed Linden dollars into savings accounts at Ginko Financial bank, hoping to earn the promised double-digit interest. Some did, but in July there was a run on the bank and panic spread as Ginko A.T.M.'s eventually stopped giving depositors their money back. The bank has since vanished. With no official law and order in Second Life, investors have little recourse.

Robert J. Bloomfield, a behavioral economist at Cornell University, studies investor behavior in the real world and recently became interested in how investors behave similarly in Second Life. "We know the little guy makes lots of dumb mistakes," Professor Bloomfield said. "They tend to be overly impressed by the trappings of success. We see that magnified in Second Life."

Some Second Life residents are calling for in-world regulatory agencies — the user-run Second Life Exchange Commission has just begun operating — and some expect real-world institutions to become involved as the Second Life population and economy expands. "It's a horse race as to whether the I.R.S. or S.E.C. will start noticing first," Mr. Duranske said.

It's Love at First Kill

BY STEPHANIE ROSENBLOOM | APRIL 22, 2011

THIS IS A LOVE STORY. It began on a hot summer night in Santa Barbara, Calif., when Tamara Langman helped kill the yellow-eyed demon known as Prince Malchezaar. She was logged into World of Warcraft, the multiplayer fantasy game, and her avatar — Arixi Fizzlebolt, a busty gnome with three blond pigtails — had also managed to pique the interest of John Bentley, a k a Weulfgar McDoal.

A note to the uninitiated: World of Warcraft is a vast online game where monsters are meant to be vanquished, but it is also a social networking experience. When players aren't battling monsters, their avatars are exploring fantastical landscapes (lush jungles, snowy forests, misty beaches), where they can meet and gab via the game's instant message feature, or through voice communication software.

And so Ms. Langman and Mr. Bentley found a quiet spot for their avatars to sit. Hours evaporated as they discussed everything from their families to their futures. Sometime before dawn, Ms. Langman realized that while she was in the fictional world of Azeroth, she was also on a date.

For the next two months, Ms. Langman, 27, and Mr. Bentley, 24, rendezvoused in Azeroth, until one day they decided to meet in Santa Barbara instead. When Mr. Bentley stepped onto the tarmac at the Santa Barbara airport on a bright October afternoon in 2008, Ms. Langman ran to him. Mr. Bentley scooped her up into his arms and spun her around.

He had planned to stay for a couple of weeks before returning to Atlanta. But two weeks became two years, and Mr. Bentley and Ms. Langman are still together.

Who knew a World of Warcraft subscription could deliver more romance than Match.com?

Tamara Langman and her boyfriend met as avatars.

Ms. Langman and Mr. Bentley are hardly the only couple to have forged an avatar love connection. Gaming forums are rife with anecdotes from players who are dating and marrying. Some couples have even had their avatars marry. (You can watch videos of the ceremonies on YouTube.)

And while it may sound like something out of a science fiction novel, more people are likely to meet this way as the genre (known as massively multiplayer online role-playing games, or MMORPGs) continues to grow. With more than 12 million subscribers, World of Warcraft is one of the most popular games of its kind in the world (others include EverQuest, Aion, Guild Wars). That's a sizable dating pool. Match.com, by way of comparison, has fewer than 2 million subscribers.

"It's giving people something that they're missing in the real world," said Ramona Pringle, an interactive media producer and a professor of new media at the Ryerson School of Image Arts in Toronto. "It is a really primal experience. It's about survival. It's about needing someone."

Ms. Pringle, 29, first observed gamer love connections while working as an interactive producer for the PBS "Frontline" project called "Digital Nation." At BlizzCon 2009, a gaming convention in California, she was stunned by the number of die-hard gamers holding hands and pushing baby carriages.

She thought about her friends: successful, striking and yet struggling to find love. She herself — willowy with wide green eyes — had just had a breakup with a boyfriend. "What's going on that these people we consider the fringe, these gamers, are finding love?" she said, nursing a beer at a bar in Austin, Tex., last month during the South by Southwest Interactive conference. She wanted to see what gaming might teach her about love.

So instead of turning to religion or therapy to mend her heart, Ms. Pringle said, she turned to World of Warcraft.

More than 40 percent of online gamers are women, and adult women are among the industry's fastest growing demographics, representing 33 percent of the game-playing population — a larger portion than boys 17 and younger, who make up 20 percent, according to the Entertainment Software Association, an industry group.

To help her navigate World of Warcraft, Ms. Pringle enlisted Brent George, the animation director for James Cameron's Avatar: The Game, to be her guide. They began playing last summer — she from Toronto, he from Montreal — as many as six hours a night.

As Ms. Pringle tumbled down the rabbit hole, she found herself directing her avatar — Tristanova, a graceful blue-skinned night elf priest — to run excitedly up to Mr. George's avatar, Caethis, a heroic-looking warrior. "It's remarkable to me that you can have a crush on someone's avatar," Ms. Pringle said.

But she did. The two have never been romantically involved, yet when Mr. George told her that he would be her knight in shining armor, "I have to admit, my heart skipped a beat," she said, "even though we hadn't met in person."

Ramona Pringle, above, gave a presentation on Warcraft at South by Southwest.

Multiplayer games encourage such alliances. The beginner's guide to World of Warcraft notes that you can go it alone, "but by going it alone, you won't be able to master some of the game's tougher challenges, you will likely take longer to reach the endgame, and you won't have access to the game's most powerful magical treasures." Ms. Pringle thinks that is analogous to love.

"We have a society that's really built upon self-sufficiency and independence and yet it's not sustainable," she said. "You need someone with your complementary skills to get through it."

Take Hannah Romero of Vancouver. When her avatar, Cosomina, met an avatar named Dreadmex (he's Mexican American), she was unimpressed. His opening line was something to the effect of "Whazzup, homeys?"

But later, when the avatars both showed up early to a group raid, they made small talk. Ms. Romero said that it began as innocent elevator-type chatter but that over time, Cosomina fell for Dreadmex.

They became inseparable, spending hours lounging beside by waterfalls and strolling through parks.

Yet why communicate through avatars? Why not pick up the phone? Or Skype?

"When you're talking on the phone you can say all of those things, but there's no physicality to it," said Ms. Romero, a food services director for a gaming company. "And in the game, even though somebody's 2,000 miles away, they've made an effort to sit down and hold your hand. Even though it's not real, the emotion of it is real."

Speaking of emotions, the first time she let Dreadmex know she loved him, she did so in the game, and then swiftly logged off. "You can say 'I love you' and then run away," Ms. Romero said. "That moment — 'Should I tell somebody I love them?' — it's a big deal, right? So to be able to say it and then to disappear is pretty great."

Other gamers have echoed that sentiment, saying that typing their feelings or flirtations is less awkward than saying them aloud. That can lead to more-honest conversations, and fewer misunderstandings. It's why many players believe that they come to know each other faster and better than, say, people who meet over a few dates.

Eventually, the woman who created Cosomina flew to Los Angeles to meet Pete Romero, the man behind Dreadmex. Like many people who meet on the Internet, she momentarily panicked. "That little voice in my head is like 'Are you crazy?' " she said.

But there was no need to worry. The couple spent the weekend eating, perusing vinyl records, walking on the beach. A year later, on March 27, 2010, they married.

While these stories seem like fairy tales, gamers insist they're not.

"I love my husband a great deal," said Ms. Romero, who noted that despite her love story, she's a mother, a career woman and "obviously not a nut." "The reality is we're not magic. We don't live in a game. We live in a real life. The dishes still need to get done."

Meeting online eliminates some of the reasons people never pursue each other, be it an awkward first date or a bad hair day.

Still, psychologists and sociologists say there does appear to be a connection between gamers and the avatars they choose. "Most players say the avatar they created instinctually is most like them," said Ms. Pringle, who created a World of Warcraft personality guide based on gamer interviews, studies of archetypes and the Myers-Briggs Type Indicator (at avatarsecrets.com). She also has a television pilot in development about the blurry line between virtual and real worlds.

As for Ms. Langman and Mr. Bentley, they live in Mississippi, though at the moment Ms. Langman is in St. Louis. (As a costume designer and draper for theatrical productions, she's often on the road.) Mr. Bentley counts bills at a casino, a job he landed through a fellow gamer in World of Warcraft. "I don't see how he could have gotten this job opportunity without World of Warcraft," Ms. Langman said.

He wouldn't have gotten Ms. Langman, either. "There's something magical about falling in love with someone just through writing and then waiting for a reply," said Ms. Langman, for whom Mr. Bentley once stormed a castle. "It's evocative of ancient romances where pen-and-ink love letters were delivered on horseback. Just the kind of forgotten world that Warcraft seeks to recreate in digital space."

It's the world of Arixi and Weulfgar. And in case you're wondering if, in between watching DVDs and doing laundry, they still hunt monsters together in Azeroth, they do.

Said Ms. Langman: "We had a raid last night."

Four Hours of Screen Time? No Problem

BY DIANE MEHTA | NOV. 16, 2012

THIS PAST SUMMER, I came home from work to find my son and his friend M. playing Roblox, a massively multiplayer online game that lets you construct virtual worlds and customize an avatar to explore it.

"How long have they been playing?" I asked his baby sitter.

"Four hours," she said.

Stunned, I looked at them. "Four?"

At 8 ½, my son had a 15-minute daily limit for iPod games or the Wii and 30 minutes on weekends. By all rights, I should want to kill my baby sitter, who knew that. But I looked at my son, happy, hands flying over the keyboard, talking and laughing with his new friend, and realized, I didn't care.

It was his first play date in months. There were extenuating circumstances. Over the course of second grade, his behavior deteriorated so badly that he lost every single friend. I looked at his baby sitter and shrugged. "They're happy," she confirmed.

The possibility of a new friendship emerging, for me, outweighed all the warnings about screen time.

I knew the arguments about how children learned. I wasn't unaware of the impact of wasting time online and the results of a Kaiser Family Foundation survey, which pegged children's media use at 7 hours and 38 minutes daily. I tried not to think about the developmental impact of technology on brain chemistry.

I looked at the computer. My son had built himself a big house with secret passageways to explore a grassy roof, a pool and roller coasters all over. M. helped him design his avatar. Then my son invited M.'s avatar over. Roblox wasn't a shoot-'em-up game. There was no violence, no sex. He was laughing. My hopefulness outweighed my guilt. The game was giving him a way into friendship.

A year and a half earlier, my husband and I told him we were getting divorced. Except for a grunting tic, severe at home but tamped down at school, he held it together through first grade, a model student.

In second grade, he unraveled. He became more unsettled and uncontrollably hyperactive. Twice a week, he struggled to reconcile the excitement of seeing one parent with the sadness of leaving the other.

He struggled socially. He lost friend after friend. Play dates became loaded because we anticipated the inevitably disappointing outcome. When one play date didn't go well, he said repeatedly how terrible it was, nervous the girl would agree but hoping she wouldn't. She refused to see him again. With a girl who had been his best friend for years, he was so impulsive that their play dates also ended.

And in that delicate time when boys begin to search out same-sex friendships, he was lost. He was unable to staunch the flow of rude or impulsive comments to others, and he could not absorb the consequences. He had no filter. He fell in with a group of troublemakers, finding it easier to join the trouble rather than risk another real friendship.

Like most children, he had plenty to say and thousands of questions. But he was different. He couldn't stop talking. "It's like a motor," his teacher said, he just can't turn off, and it lasted the entire day.

But while playing Roblox with M., he quieted down. The structure of the game constricted his behavior to imaginative activities in that particular environment. For a child with a fast mind and the verbal expansiveness of a kid much older than himself, the strictures of the massively multiplayer game helped structure the friendship he was building. For the first time all year, he took advice without falling apart; he gave M. a chance to speak. He wasn't doing all the talking.

Roblox wasn't a fast-moving or overstimulating game, and when my son was playing it, he had no problem following instructions. He was able to sit down. The game seemed to neutralize his seemingly intractable problems and thus invited the possibility of a friendship.

I also knew, from a stint in consulting, the limits of surveys. The Kaiser survey double-counted for multitasking. So listening to music while using the computer was counted separately. I remembered how my son's tutor said to put on background music to combat the distraction of silence while he tackled his assignments. And I stopped worrying about the survey.

Maybe massively multiplayer games weren't so bad, either. A 2006 article by Constance Steinkuehler and Dmitri Williams said such games were the latest iteration of fantasy and science-fiction books ("The Hobbit") and games ("Dungeons and Dragons"), with their open-ended narratives. My son was a child who questioned what others took for granted. Roblox not only let him explore the world and build stuff to put in it, but it was giving his real life a new narrative.

Over the summer, I let my son and M. play as much as they wanted. In between game time, they threw a rubber ball relentlessly at the building. I whittled down their game time. I took them out for ice cream. We went on a bike ride. They sat on the stairs and hung out, bored, an activity I considered useful. True, he was still logging dozens and dozens of hours of Roblox over an alarmingly short period.

But he had made a friend. And instead of worrying, I was overjoyed.

Disruptions: Minecraft, an Obsession and an Educational Tool

BY NICK BILTON | SEPT. 15, 2013

IF YOU WERE to walk into my sister's house in Los Angeles, you'd hear a bit of yelling from time to time. "Luca! Get off Minecraft! Luca, are you on Minecraft again? Luca! Enough with the Minecraft!"

Luca is my 8-year-old nephew. Like millions of other children his age, Luca is obsessed with the video game Minecraft. Actually, obsessed might be an understated way to explain a child's idée fixe with the game. And my sister, whom you've probably guessed is the person doing all that yelling, is a typical parent of a typical Minecraft-playing child: she's worried it might be rotting his brain.

For those who have never played Minecraft, it's relatively simple. The game looks a bit crude because it doesn't have realistic graphics. Instead, it's built in 16-bit, a computer term that means the graphics look blocky, like giant, digital Lego pieces.

Unlike other video games, there are few if any instructions in Minecraft. Instead, like the name suggests, the goal of the game is to craft, or build, structures in these 16-bit worlds, and figuring things out on your own is a big part of it. And parents, it's not terribly violent. Sure, you can kill a few zombies while playing in the game's "survival mode." But in its "creative mode," Minecraft is about building, exploration, creativity and even collaboration.

The game was first demonstrated by Markus Persson, a Swedish video game programmer and designer known as Notch, in 2009 and released to the public in November 2011. Today, the game runs on various devices, including desktop computers, Google Android smartphones, Apple iOS and the Microsoft Xbox. There are thousands of mods, or modifications, for the game, that allow people to play in prebuilt worlds, like a replica of Paris (Eiffel Tower included) or an ancient Mayan civilization.

While parents — my sister included — might worry that all these pixels and the occasional zombie might be bad for children, a lot of experts say they shouldn't fret.

Earlier this year, for example, a school in Stockholm made Minecraft compulsory for 13-year-old students. "They learn about city planning, environmental issues, getting things done, and even how to plan for the future," said Monica Ekman, a teacher at the Viktor Rydberg school.

Around the world, Minecraft is being used to educate children on everything from science to city planning to speaking a new language, said Joel Levin, co-founder and education director at the company TeacherGaming. TeacherGaming runs MinecraftEdu, which is intended to help teachers use the game with students.

A history teacher in Australia set up "quest missions" where students can wander through and explore ancient worlds. An English-language teacher in Denmark told children they could play Minecraft collectively in the classroom but with one caveat: they were allowed to communicate both orally and through text only in English. A science teacher in California has set up experiments in Minecraft to teach students about gravity.

Mr. Levin said that in addition to classroom exercises, children were learning the digital skills they would need as they got older.

"Kids are getting into middle school and high school and having some ugly experiences on Facebook and other social networks without an understanding of how to interact with people online," he said. "With Minecraft, they are developing that understanding at a very early age."

While there are no known neuroscience studies of Minecraft's effect on children's brains, research has shown video games can have a positive impact on children.

A study by S.R.I. International, a Silicon Valley research group that specializes in technology, found that game-based play could raise cognitive learning for students by as much as 12 percent and improve hand-eye coordination, problem-solving ability and memory.

Games like Minecraft also encourage what researchers call "parallel play," where children are engrossed in their game but are still connected through a server or are sharing the same screen. And children who play games could even become better doctors. No joke. Neuroscientists performed a study at Iowa State University that found that surgeons performed better, and were more accurate on the operating table, when they regularly played video games.

"Minecraft extends kids' spatial reasoning skills, construction skills and understanding of planning," said Eric Klopfer, a professor and the director of the Massachusetts Institute of Technology's Scheller Teacher Education Program. "In many ways, it's like a digital version of Lego."

Professor Klopfer suggested that if parents were worried about the game, they should simply play it with their children. He said he set up a server in his house so his children's friends could play together and he could monitor their behavior and then explain that some actions, even in virtual worlds, are unethical — like destroying someone's Minecraft house, or calling them a bad name.

But Professor Klopfer warned that, as with anything, there was — probably to my nephew's chagrin — such as thing as too much Minecraft.

"While the game is clearly good for kids, it doesn't mean there should be no limits," he said. "As with anything, I don't want my kids to do any one thing for overly extended periods of time. Whether Legos or Minecraft; having limits is an important part their learning."

Many children would happily ignore that little warning if their parents let them.

Last weekend, my sister saw Luca on his computer with what appeared to be Minecraft on the screen. "Luca, I told you, you can't play Minecraft anymore," she said.

"I'm not playing Minecraft, mama," he replied. "I'm watching videos on YouTube of other people playing Minecraft."

Behind League of Legends, E-Sports's Main Attraction

BY DAVID SEGAL | OCT. 10, 2014

WHEN THE COMPANY behind one of the world's most popular video games, League of Legends, started organizing tournaments — noisy events where professional players compete under huge screens in arenas packed with fans — it had to design a championship trophy. That proved trickier than it sounds. A trophy should be grand and gleaming — that much seemed obvious. But nobody at Riot Games, which owns League of Legends, focused on a pretty basic question: How much should the trophy weigh?

While there are many correct answers, it turns out that "about 70 pounds" isn't one of them. Seventy pounds is roughly twice as heavy as hockey's Stanley Cup, and hockey players, if we can generalize for a moment, tend to be brawnier than gamers.

"It takes five people to hoist it," said Dustin Beck, a vice president at Riot Games. He was sitting in the company's offices in Santa Monica, Calif., and talking about what is officially known as the Summoner's Cup, an oversize silver-plated chalice that looks like a faintly sinister "Game of Thrones" prop. "We thought we'd be able to send it back to Thomas Lyte" — the British company that fabricated it — "and they shaved like five pounds off. Still not enough."

Though the Summoner's Cup may be too weighty to lift in victory, it is coveted by the several hundred professionals who play League of Legends full time.

Dozens of those players are now in Seoul, at the fourth world championship. On Oct. 19, the finals will be held in a stadium built for soccer's World Cup, with 40,000 fans expected and many times that number watching online. Last year, Riot Games says, 32 million people around the world saw a South Korean team win the Summoner's Cup, along with a grand prize of $1 million, in the Staples Center in Los

The Summoner's Cup awaited the top team at the League of Legends World Champion-ships, which are being held this month before cheering crowds in Busan, South Korea.

Angeles. That's an audience larger than the one that tuned in to the last game of the N.B.A. finals that year.

Since its debut in 2009, League of Legends has evolved from a small population of desktop-computer warriors into a full-scale phenomenon. In the process, it has become an e-sport. If you are not a male between the ages of 15 and 25, a group that Riot says accounts for 90 percent of all LoL players, the odds are good that you have never heard of e-sports, a catchall term for games that resemble conventional sports insofar as they have superstars, playoffs, fans, uniforms, comebacks and upsets. But all the action in e-sports occurs online, and the contestants hardly move.

In the case of League of Legends, players work a keyboard and a mouse, wielding exotic weapons in a virtual forest of turrets and torches, apparently landscaped by refugees of "Lord of the Rings." The standard match is a mercilessly kinetic and bewilderingly complex battle between two teams of five players; each team tries to destroy the other's nexus, a gaudy purple structure that glows like a mood ring.

Though e-sports were around for about a decade before Riot Games was born, no company has jumped in with the same intensity. Riot controls every aspect of the professional league, right down to the music composed for live events. It runs tournaments worldwide, with its own slick broadcasting operation streaming to various Internet video sites, complete with color commentators and highlight reels — a kind of ESPN for gamers. The company also keeps a few hundred professional players on salary, ensuring that they can spend up to 14 hours a day practicing, the time required to compete at the highest level. Today, according to SuperData, a market research firm, League of Legends has more than eight times the number of active players as Dota 2, its closest rival in the genre known as multiplayer online battle arena.

Yet despite ticket prices of $15 to $50 for seats at league events, the league itself is a money loser. The tournaments function as marketing to bring in new players and to inspire loyalty in regulars, says Marc Merrill, a Riot Games co-founder and the company president. The goal is to inspire enthusiasts, doing for LoL what LeBron James and other stars do for basketball.

Which is just the first reason that Riot Games' business model sounds insane, at least initially. The second is that the game is free to play and can be downloaded from the Internet, with no special hardware required. And players can't buy extra power or skill for their online avatars, known as "champions" in LoL parlance. In other words, you could play League of Legends for years and never spend a nickel.

What the company sells to anyone playing the game — and, for the moment, it sells them nothing else — are game enhancements and goodies that cost less than $10 apiece. This may not seem like a path to riches, but if the player base is big and riveted enough, it is. The company says there are now 67 million active monthly players around the world, and in August alone this crowd spent $122 million, according to SuperData.

"Whenever I talk to executives at Riot, it's like a mantra: 'Revenue is second, the player experience is first,' " said Joost van Dreunen, chief executive of SuperData. "The paradox is that by putting revenue second, League will be one of the very few games to bring in $1 billion in 2014."

$2 HERE, $7.50 THERE

Riot Games' offices are spread around three buildings in an industrial park, and in a handful of satellite offices around the world. About 1,500 people work at the company, most of them in the Santa Monica location. The place looks like a snack-filled haven for young slackers, with lots of employees in flip-flops and T-shirts, but attention to detail defines the company. One wall has a list of dos and don'ts for presenting Riot's logo, a clenched fist. "The fist should never look like it's passive, retreating or hanging on for dear life," is among the don'ts.

Another sign of mindfulness: The window shades along walls facing east are usually drawn, even on a recent sunny day.

"Oh, yeah, security concern," said Brandon Beck, the company's chief executive, taking a seat in his office, illuminated mostly by overhead lights at 3:30 in the afternoon. "Occasionally we have confidential stuff on the walls here and we've had snoopers outside with, like, telescopic lenses."

Mr. Beck, who is a co-founder of the company with Mr. Merrill and is also Dustin Beck's older brother, is a slight guy with a dark beard who rarely stops smiling. He and Mr. Merrill got to know each other through gaming circles while attending rival private high schools in the Los Angeles area.

As teenagers, both were fans of online, text-based versions of Dungeons & Dragons, and both monopolized the phone lines in their homes back in the dial-up days of the Internet. As game graphics improved, the two moved on to so-called real-time strategy games like Starcraft and Warcraft II. Other games required expensive consoles like Xbox or PlayStation, and in many cases developers had little incentive to fine-tune or expand these games after an initial run of sales. That's because they made money by offering a $60 sequel on disc or, in other cases, through subscriptions.

"It was always disappointing when development teams would rush in to build the next game and neglect communities that were staying engaged with their game well after it launched," Mr. Beck said. "We wanted a company that paid attention to players like us who wanted to play competitively and cooperatively."

If the ideal game didn't exist, these two were going to help create it. Both attended the University of Southern California, and after a failed venture with another game maker, they decided to start a company of their own. In 2006, they moved into the cheapest space they could rent, a mechanical engineering lab in West Los Angeles, and opened Riot Games. Eventually, they won over about two dozen angel investors from Benchmark Capital and FirstMark Capital, then severely tried the patience of those investors.

"We thought it would cost $3 million to build League of Legends," Mr. Merrill said. "It ended up costing six times that."

When League of Legends went live, in October 2009, the free-to-play model was little loved in the United States, where it was associated with lame graphics and money cadging. (Players were constantly begged for dollars.) But in Asia, free-to-play companies were raking in so much cash that subscription games were unplugging, temporarily, so they could re-emerge later as giveaways.

Four months after League of Legends was introduced, 20,000 people were playing it simultaneously.

"Within 90 days you could see the bone structure of a hit," said Mitch Lasky, then a board member and a Benchmark Capital investor. "It was doing small numbers at first, but if you knew where to look — how many people were coming in, how many games they played, revenue per average user — you could see the first couple hundred million in revenue."

Then as now, Riot collects money when players spend small sums — in the range of $2 to $7.50 — to acquire champions that they control during the game. They can also buy "skins," which are modifications to those champions. Care for a Halloween-themed version of a champion named Vlad? How about a champion named French Maid Nidalee reimagined as a white tiger? They are for sale.

"People told us when we started that if you don't charge up front, or if you're not selling extra power or stats, it won't work," Mr. Merrill said. "But that fails to account for the coolness factor. If you're really into cars, you don't mind spending $50,000 to soup up your Honda. That's the player we're tapping into."

The active user base would grow so fast that Riot Games scrambled to expand the infrastructure and keep up with demand. In 2011, a majority stake in the company was acquired by the Chinese gaming giant Tencent for more than $350 million, according to a Bloomberg report. Riot's e-sport initiative had yet to take off, but when the deal was announced, LoL had more than two million monthly active users and a fan base that skewed Asian. Today, 80 percent of players are in Asia, according to Riot, and in Korea there's a nightly League of Legends TV show.

Mr. Merrill and Mr. Beck had never owned the company, because, as Mr. Merrill put it, they weren't very savvy deal makers when they started. But they say they have autonomy and a great relationship with Tencent.

"They told us, 'We want to buy you so that nobody else does and messes up the company,' " Mr. Merrill said.

BLITZCRANKS AND POWER FISTS

At its most basic level, League of Legends is a game of capture the flag, though that is a bit like describing brain surgery as "a medical procedure."

Before play begins, the 10 members of two teams each select a champion, each with a distinct personality, back story and powers. Jinx, for example, is a blue-haired vixen who "likes to wreak havoc without a thought for the consequences, leaving a trail of mayhem and panic in her wake," as it says on the League of Legends website. Jinx has a minigun named Pow-Pow and a rocket launcher named Fish-bones, both of which inflict a very specific type of damage.

So the first step to LoL expertise is memorizing the abilities of every champion — all 120 of them.

And counting. League of Legends has been engineered to be as engrossing as possible; the company prefers the word "engaging" because it insists that "engrossing" has negative connotation. Part of that engineering involves constant tinkering. New champions are issued every month or so, and the powers of longstanding champions can be reduced ("nerfed" in LoL lingo) or enhanced ("buffed") by Riot Games.

"There are regular updates to the game," said Joedat Esfahani, a professional player who competes under the name Voyboy. "That forces everyone to rethink their strategy and figure out the optimal way to play. It's a race to innovate. The best teams are the ones that are constantly evolving along with the game."

Riot likes to say LoL is easy to learn but impossible to master. That's half right. Even the online tutorial that greets you after sign-up will make a neophyte break into a sweat. A woman's voice explains the basics of LoL mechanics and iconography, a barrage of information that is hard to hear over the foreboding soundtrack. As you zoom around a verdant battleground called Summoner's Rift as if strapped to an overhead camera, you're supposed to read a lot of instruction text at the same time.

If you don't do this fast enough, you are ejected from the tutorial and admonished for being pokey. Speed matters. The eye-hand coordination is so tricky that, according to Riot, pros over 25 years old start to age out of the top rungs of the league.

Those who manage to digest the language and arcana of LoL will swear that the following sentence, spoken by the panting narrator of a recent plays-of-the-week video, makes perfect sense:

"She kites Blitzcrank through the creeps staying perfectly out of range to avoid the Power Fist and take him down as she flashes to make it a double."

Riot Games has bucked one of the most unbuckable trends of the digital age. Instead of chopping stuff into timesaving bits — turning information into listicles, à la BuzzFeed, or limiting videos to six seconds, à la Vine — League of Legends demands dozens of hours to attain even a basic level of competence.

Given all the variables of play, it was only a matter of time before fans started developing moves that the game's creators had never imagined. In game design circles, this is known as "emergent behavior." Brandon Beck remembers when he first saw it in LoL, in a YouTube video in which a player made an improbable escape, then baited the enemy into a chase that led directly into the clutches of his teammates.

"He was leveraging the mechanics of the game in ways that we didn't even predict," Mr. Beck said, still marveling. "We actually showed that play to everyone in the company at a weekly meeting we call show and tell, and everyone was left awe-struck."

A professional league wasn't originally a core part of Riot's business plan, though the co-founders thought from the start that they had created a game as fun to watch as any sport. The league became a focus in 2011, after Riot held its first championship tournament at DreamHack, a twice-a-year computer festival in Sweden. Several hundred thousand people watched online, via Twitch.tv, far surpassing the company's expectations.

Viewership has since soared, and the league has expanded. Next year, the company will stage multiple matches, every week, in more than a half-dozen countries. There are professional teams with their own managers, sponsors, sports psychologists and increasingly contentious relationships with their star players, many of whom earn six figures through salaries, endorsements and tournaments.

"A lot of money is now funneled through e-sports," said Steve Arhancet, who owns Team Curse, one of the most successful squads based in the United States. "When I negotiate a contract with one of my players now, it's my lawyer talking to his lawyer. It wasn't like that two years ago."

The finals on October 19th will be held in a stadium built for soccer's World Cup, with 40,000 fans expected and many times that number watching online.

THE WEATHER IN SHURIMA

In mid-September, six people met in a room at Riot Games. They were members of a corporate division, called Foundations, tasked with fleshing out the history of all the game's champions, including the climate, landscape, architecture and dress of their place of origin.

Little of that information has any effect on game play. The point of Foundations is to lend concreteness to the Legends universe, as it's depicted for fans on the website and in promotional materials.

A new champion, Azir, had just been unveiled. He comes from a place called Shurima, a once-grand empire in a sweltering desert. The Foundations team looked at Shurima images from the art department, projected on a large video screen.

"The designs on the sword look great, but I want to think about leather," said a team member, looking at the leather garb of a Shurima soldier. "In this environment, I think leather is not your friend."

"It'd be minimal," someone else agreed.

"You'd cook in it," said another.

While Foundations spends its days refining aesthetics and narratives, a separate group is devoted to policing online player etiquette. It's a problem facing just about every video game publisher. When a few million males in their teens and 20s get together and try to slaughter one another online, in an anonymous setting, while able to chat via on-screen texts, slurs are inevitable.

A few years ago, Riot Games trawled academia for hard-core gamers to lead a player behavior team. The company hired Jeffrey Lin, who was working on a Ph.D. in cognitive neuroscience at the University of Washington. He and his colleagues set up a kind of community policing system for flagging offensive conduct or speech and voting on whether the flagged player should receive a warning. Warned players who didn't reform were banned for two weeks, or, if the infractions were numerous or bad enough, permanently.

"Online society has developed without consequences," Mr. Lin said. "If you were homophobic or used a racial slur, nobody punished you for it."

Mr. Lin says 75 percent of players who receive a warning immediately change their behavior. But the rate of recidivism was high enough that in July, he announced tougher sanctions via Twitter. Henceforth, he wrote, "players that show extreme toxicity," which includes homophobic and racist language, as well as death threats, "will be instantly 14-day or permabanned."

The next day, Mr. Lin reported on Twitter that he had been inundated with racist tweets.

While Riot Games is combating noxious talk, critics contend that it all but encourages a type of sexism. A website called League of Sexism critiques, among other things, female champions — who tend to be male fantasies of slim, busty women in extravagantly kinky outfits — and their images as presented in paintings, called splash art, that are posted to the LoL site.

A Riot Games producer, Omar Kendall, addressed this issue at the Comic-Con convention in July, by saying, in effect, that the company was working on it. But the splash art for a champion named Shyvana, who has improbable proportions and a lot of bare skin, was posted just a few weeks ago, suggesting that this new body-type strategy isn't exactly urgent.

Or perhaps it's just low on a list of priorities. Riot Games feels like a company in a full-out sprint. It is now enhancing the production values of its world championship, hoping to make more of the sort of corporate sponsorship deals that could transform the league from loss leader into moneymaker. Coca-Cola and Korean Air are currently on board.

The company is also working on an online merchandise store, to open in 2015, which for the first time will sell official League of Legends items — T-shirts, sweaters and track jackets. One million pieces, in 40 to 50 categories, will be offered. When the store opens, Riot expects hundreds of thousands of clicks every second on the LoL site, roughly the traffic whenever champions are introduced.

"That's about what Target sees on its site on Black Friday," said Dustin Beck, who is also in charge of the e-store.

If the past is any indication, traffic on opening day will surpass even these ambitious expectations. At every step, Riot has underestimated the appeal of its game, from how fast it would catch on, to how much people would spend, to the rise of its e-sports league. It is a gaming company run by gamers who constantly ask, "What would I want from this game?" and then provide it, even if it won't yield immediate profits.

At its root, this means fretting over minutiae, like what soldiers wear in Shurima, the power of Jinx's minigun and, of course, the weight of the Summoner's Cup. No matter who wins next weekend in Seoul, rest assured that the thing will be sent back to Thomas Lyte again and forced to lose some weight.

The Minecraft Generation

BY CLIVE THOMPSON | APRIL 14, 2016

JORDAN WANTED TO build an unpredictable trap.

An 11-year-old in dark horn-rimmed glasses, Jordan is a devotee of Minecraft, the computer game in which you make things out of virtual blocks, from dizzying towers to entire cities. He recently read "The Maze Runner," a sci-fi thriller in which teenagers live inside a booby-trapped labyrinth, and was inspired to concoct his own version — something he then would challenge his friends to navigate.

Jordan built a variety of obstacles, including a deluge of water and walls that collapsed inward, Indiana Jones-style. But what he really wanted was a trap that behaved unpredictably. That would really throw his friends off guard. How to do it, though? He obsessed over the problem.

Then it hit him: the animals! Minecraft contains a menagerie of virtual creatures, some of which players can kill and eat (or tame, if they want pets). One, a red-and-white cowlike critter called a mooshroom, is known for moseying about aimlessly. Jordan realized he could harness the animal's movement to produce randomness. He built a pen out of gray stones and installed "pressure plates" on the floor that triggered a trap inside the maze. He stuck the mooshroom inside, where it would totter on and off the plates in an irregular pattern.

Presto: Jordan had used the cow's weird behavior to create, in effect, a random-number generator inside Minecraft. It was an ingenious bit of problem-solving, something most computer engineers I know would regard as a great hack — a way of coaxing a computer system to do something new and clever.

When I visited Jordan at his home in New Jersey, he sat in his family's living room at dusk, lit by a glowing iMac screen, and mused on Minecraft's appeal. "It's like the earth, the world, and you're the creator of it," he said. On-screen, he steered us over to the entrance to the maze, and I peered in at the contraptions chugging away. "My art teacher always says, 'No games are creative, except for the people who create them.' But she said, 'The only exception that I have for that is Minecraft.'" He floated over to the maze's exit, where he had posted a sign for the survivors: *The journey matters more than what you get in the end.*

Since its release seven years ago, Minecraft has become a global sensation, captivating a generation of children. There are over 100 million registered players, and it's now the third-best-selling video game in history, after Tetris and Wii Sports. In 2014, Microsoft bought Minecraft — and Mojang, the Swedish game studio behind it — for $2.5 billion.

There have been blockbuster games before, of course. But as Jordan's experience suggests — and as parents peering over their children's shoulders sense — Minecraft is a different sort of phenomenon.

For one thing, it doesn't really feel like a game. It's more like a destination, a technical tool, a cultural scene, or all three put together: a place where kids engineer complex machines, shoot videos of their escapades that they post on YouTube, make art and set up servers, online versions of the game where they can hang out with friends. It's a world of trial and error and constant discovery, stuffed with byzantine secrets, obscure text commands and hidden recipes. And it runs completely counter to most modern computing trends. Where companies like Apple and Microsoft and Google want our computers to be easy to manipulate — designing point-and-click interfaces under the assumption that it's best to conceal from the average user how the computer works — Minecraft encourages kids to get under the hood, break things, fix them and turn mooshrooms into random-number generators. It invites them to tinker.

In this way, Minecraft culture is a throwback to the heady early days of the digital age. In the late '70s and '80s, the arrival of personal computers like the Commodore 64 gave rise to the first generation of kids fluent in computation. They learned to program in Basic, to write software that they swapped excitedly with their peers. It was a playful renaissance that eerily parallels the embrace of Minecraft by today's youth. As Ian

Bogost, a game designer and professor of media studies at Georgia Tech, puts it, Minecraft may well be this generation's personal computer.

At a time when even the president is urging kids to learn to code, Minecraft has become a stealth gateway to the fundamentals, and the pleasures, of computer science. Those kids of the '70s and '80s grew up to become the architects of our modern digital world, with all its allures and perils. What will the Minecraft generation become?

"CHILDREN," THE SOCIAL critic Walter Benjamin wrote in 1924, "are particularly fond of haunting any site where things are being visibly worked on. They are irresistibly drawn by the detritus generated by building, gardening, housework, tailoring or carpentry."

Playing with blocks, it turns out, has deep cultural roots in Europe. Colin Fanning, a curatorial fellow at the Philadelphia Museum of Art, points out that European philosophers have long promoted block-based games as a form of "good" play that cultivates abstract thought. A recent paper Fanning wrote with Rebecca Mir traces the tradition to the English political philosopher John Locke, who was an early advocate of alphabet blocks. A century later, Friedrich Froebel — often called the inventor of kindergarten — developed block-based toys that he claimed would illustrate the spiritual connectedness of all things. Children would start with simple blocks, build up to more complex patterns, then begin to see these patterns in the world around them. Educators like Maria Montessori picked up on this concept and pioneered the teaching of math through wooden devices.

During the political cataclysms of the 20th century, European thinkers regarded construction-play not merely as a way to educate children but also as a means to heal their souls. The Danish landscape architect Carl Theodor Sorensen urged that areas in cities ruined by World War II be turned into "junk playgrounds," where children would be given pickaxes, hammers and saws and allowed to shape the detritus into a new civilization, at child scale. (Several were in fact created in Europe and were quite popular.) In Sweden, educators worried that industrialization and the mechanization of society were causing children to lose touch with physical skills; they began teaching *sloyd*, or woodcrafting, a practice that continues today.

When Fanning first saw Minecraft, he felt a jolt of recognition. Nearly all these historical impulses were evident in the game. "It's striking to me how much this mirrors the appeal and the critical reception of Minecraft," he says. "In Scandinavian toys, the material of wood has had a really long association with notions of timelessness and quality and craftsmanship." In Minecraft, as he notes, wood is one of the first resources new players gather upon entering the game: chopping trees with their avatar's hand produces blocks of wood, and from those they begin to build a civilization. Children are turned loose with tools to transform a hostile environment into something they can live in.

Block-play was, in the European tradition, regarded as a particularly "wholesome" activity; it's not hard to draw a line from that to many parents' belief that Minecraft is the "good" computer game in a world full of anxiety about too much "screen time." In this way, Minecraft has succeeded Lego as the respectable creative toy. When it was first sold in the postwar period, Lego presented itself as the heir to the heritage of playing with blocks. (One ad read: "It's a pleasure to see children playing with Lego — Lego play is quiet and stimulating. Children learn to grapple with major tasks and solve them together.") Today many cultural observers argue that Lego has moved away from that open-ended engagement, because it's so often sold in branded kits: the Hogwarts castle from "Harry Potter," the TIE fighter from "Star Wars."

"It's 'Buy the box, open the box, turn to the instruction sheet, make the model, stick it on the shelf, buy the next box,'" the veteran game designer Peter Molyneux says in a 2012 documentary about Minecraft. "Lego used to be just a big box of bricks, and you used to take the bricks, pour them on the carpet and then make stuff. And that's exactly what Minecraft is."

As a Swede, Markus Persson, who invented Minecraft and founded Mojang, grew up amid such cultural influences and probably encountered *sloyd* in school himself. In Minecraft, Persson created what Fanning calls "a sort of digital *sloyd*."

Persson, now 36, was a child of the '80s computer scene who learned to program when he was 7 on his father's Commodore 128. By the time he was in his 20s, he was working for an online photo-album site and programming games in his spare time at home, an apartment littered with game CDs and soda bottles. He released the first version of Minecraft in 2009. The basic play is fairly simple: Each time you start a new game, Minecraft generates a unique world filled with hills, forests and lakes. Whatever the player chops at or digs into yields building blocks — trees provide wood, the earth dirt and stone. Blocks can be attached to one another to quickly produce structures. Players can also combine blocks to "craft" new items. Take some stone blocks, add a few pieces of wood, and you make a pickax, which then helps you dig more quickly and deeper, till you reach precious materials like gold, silver and diamond. "Mobs," the game's creatures ("mob" is short for "mobile"), can be used for crafting, too. Kill a spider, and you get spider silk, handy for making bows and arrows.

In its first year, Minecraft found popularity mostly among adult nerds. But sometime in late 2011, according to Alex Leavitt, a Ph.D. candidate at the University of Southern California, children discovered it, and sales of the game exploded. Today it costs $27 and sells 10,000 copies a day. (It's still popular across all age groups; according to Microsoft, the average player is between 28 and 29, and women make up nearly 40 percent of all players.) Persson frequently added new features to the game, like a "survival mode," in which every 20 minutes evening falls and monsters attack — skeletons shooting arrows, "creepers" blowing themselves up when they get close to you — forcing players to build protective shelters. ("Creative mode" is just about making things.)

Persson also made it possible for players to share their works. You could package your world as a "map" and post it online for others to download and move around in. Even more sophisticated players could modify Minecraft's code, creating new types of blocks and creatures, and then put these "mods" online for others to use. Further developments included a server version of Minecraft that lets people play together on the Internet inside the same world. These days, kids can pay as little as $5 a month to rent such a server. They can also visit much larger commercial servers capable of hosting hundreds or thousands of players simultaneously. There is no single, central server: Thousands exist worldwide.

The game was a hit. But Persson became unsettled by his fame, as well as the incessant demands of his increasingly impassioned fans — who barraged him with emails, tweets and forum posts, imploring him to add new elements to Minecraft, or complaining when he updated the game and changed something. By 2014, he'd had enough. After selling Minecraft to Microsoft, he hunkered down in a $70 million mansion in Beverly Hills and now refuses to talk about Minecraft any more.

I wanted to know whether the European tradition of block-play had influenced him, but Persson politely declined to be interviewed. Via a public reply to me on Twitter, he explained that he "sold Minecraft to get away from it."

NEARLY EVERYONE who plays Minecraft, or even watches someone else do so, remarks on its feeling of freedom: All those blocks, infinities of them! Build anything you want! Players have recreated the Taj Mahal, the U.S.S. Enterprise from "Star Trek," the entire capital city from "Game of Thrones." It's the most obvious appeal of the game. But I first started to glimpse how complex Minecraft culture can be when I saw what kids were doing with what's called "redstone," the game's virtual wiring. My two sons had begun using it: Zev, who is 8, showed me an automated "piston door" and stone gateway he built. Gabriel, who is 10, had created a "minigame" whose actions included a mechanism that dropped anvils from a height, which players on the ground had to dodge.

Redstone transports energy between blocks, like an electrical connection. Attach a block that contains power — a redstone "torch," for example, which looks like a forearm-size matchstick — to one end of a trail of redstone, and anything connected to the other end will receive power. Hit a button here, and another block shifts position over there. Persson ingeniously designed redstone in a way that mimics real-world electronics. Switches and buttons and levers turn the redstone on and off, enabling players to build what computer scientists call "logic gates." Place two Minecraft switches next to each other, connect them to redstone and suddenly you have what's known as an "AND" gate: If Switch 1 and Switch 2 are both thrown, energy flows through the redstone wire. You can also rig an "OR" gate, whereby flipping either lever energizes the wire.

These AND and OR gates are, in virtual form, the same as the circuitry you'd find inside a computer chip. They're also like the Boolean logic that programmers employ every day in their code. Together, these simple gates let Minecraft players construct machines of astonishing complexity.

One day this winter, I met Sebastian, a 14-year-old, at his home in New Jersey, where he showed off his redstone devices. One was a huge "trading post," a contraption that allows players on either side of a large wall to trade items through an automated chute. It required a large cluster of AND gates, he said, and took him several days to figure out.

"Hop down here," he said, moving down into a subterranean pit beneath the apparatus and looking around. (In Minecraft, you see the world from the viewpoint of your in-game avatar.) It was like being in the bowels of a factory: the redstone sprawled in all directions. He pointed out different parts of the wiring, rattling off components like an architect at a construction site. "Coming in from these two wires are the lever inputs from the side — and from over here, the other side. And what these do is, when they're both on, they power a piston, which pairs redstone to this block up into this tower dispenser."

Mastering redstone requires rigorously logical thinking, as well as a great deal of debugging: When your device isn't working, you have to carefully go over its circuitry to figure out what's wrong. One fifth grader I visited, Natalie, was assembling a redstone door on her iPad while I watched. But nothing happened when she flicked the "on" lever. "I did that wrong," she said with a frown, and began tracing her way through the circuit. Eventually the problem emerged: A piece of redstone was angled incorrectly, sending the current in the wrong direction.

This is what computer scientists call computational thinking, and it turns out to be one of Minecraft's powerful, if subtle, effects. The game encourages kids to regard logic and if-then statements as fun things to mess around with. It teaches them what computer coders know and wrestle with every day, which is that programs rarely function at first: The work isn't so much in writing a piece of software but in debugging it, figuring out what you did wrong and coming up with a fix.

Minecraft is thus an almost perfect game for our current educational moment, in which policy makers are eager to increase kids' interest in the "STEM" disciplines — science, technology, engineering and math. Schools and governments have spent millions on "let's get kids coding" initiatives, yet it may well be that Minecraft's impact will be greater. This is particularly striking given that the game was not designed with any educational purpose in mind. "We have never done things with that sort of intent," says Jens Bergensten, the lead Minecraft developer at Mojang and Persson's first hire. "We always made the game for ourselves."

Other Minecraft features resemble the work of software engineers even more closely. For example, programmers frequently write code and control their computers through a bare-bones interface known as the "command line," typing abstruse, text-based commands rather than pointing and clicking. Many programmers I know complain that while the point-and-click world has made computers easier to use for everyday people, it has also dumbed us down; kids don't learn the command line the way they would have back when personal-computer use emerged in the '70s and '80s. This is partly why newcomers can find programming alienating: They're not accustomed to controlling a computer using only text.

But Minecraft, rather audaciously, includes a command line and requires players to figure it out. Type "t" or "/" while playing the game, and a space appears where you can chat with other players or issue commands that alter the environment. For example, typing "/time set 0" instantly changes the time of day inside the game to daybreak; the sun suddenly appears on the horizon. Complex commands require a player to master chains of sophisticated command-line syntax.

One day last fall, I visited Gus, a seventh grader in Brooklyn. He was online with friends on a server they share together, engaging in boisterous gladiatorial combat. I watched as he typed a command to endow himself with a better weapon: "/give AdventureNerd bow 1 0 {Unbreakable:1,ench:[{id:51,lvl:1}],display:{Name:"Destiny"}}." What the command did was give a bow-and-arrow weapon to Adventure-Nerd, Gus's avatar; make the bow unbreakable; endow it with magic; and name the weapon Destiny, displayed in a tag floating over the weapon. Gus had plastered virtual sticky-notes all over his Mac's desktop listing the text commands he uses most often. Several commands can be packed into a "command block," so that clicking on the block activates them, much as clicking on a piece of software launches it.

Mimi Ito, a cultural anthropologist at the University of California, Irvine, and a founder of Connected Camps, an online program where kids play Minecraft together, has closely studied gamers and learning. Ito points out that when kids delve into this hackerlike side of the game — concocting redstone devices or creating command blocks — they often wind up consulting discussion forums online, where they get advice from adult Minecraft players. These folks are often full-time programmers who love the game, and so younger kids and teenagers wind up in conversation with professionals.

"It's one of the places where young people are engaging with more expert people who are much older than them," Ito says. These connections are transformative: Kids get a glimpse of a professional path that their schoolwork never illuminates. "An adult mentor opens up these new worlds that wouldn't be open to them," she adds. Of course, critics might worry about kids interacting with adults online in this way, but as Ito notes, when there's a productive task at hand, it's similar to how guilds have passed on knowledge for ages: knowledge-able adults mentoring young people.

Ito has also found that kids' impulse to tinker with Minecraft pushes them to master real-world technical skills. One 15-year-old boy I interviewed, Eli, became interested in making "texture packs." These are the external shells that wrap around 3-D objects in the game, like a drape thrown over a table: Change the pattern on the drape, and you can change what the object looks like. Designing texture packs prompted Eli to develop sophisticated Photoshop skills. He would talk to other texture-pack designers on Minecraft forums and get them to send him their Photoshop files so he could see how they did things. He also began teaching himself to draw. "I'd be downloading the mod," he says, "looking at the original texture and saying, 'O.K., how can I make this a little more cartoony?'" Then he would put his own designs up on the forums to get feedback, which, he discovered, was usually very polite and constructive. "The community," he says, "is very helpful."

While Minecraft rewards this sort of involvement, it can also be frustrating: Mojang updates Minecraft weekly, and sometimes new updates aren't compatible with an older version. Players complained to me about waking up to discover that their complex contraptions no longer worked. One player spent weeks assembling a giant roller coaster whose carts were powered by redstone tracks only to have an update change the way rails functioned, and the entire roller-coaster mechanism never worked again. Others ruefully described spending months crafting cities on their own multiplayer servers, only to have a server crash and destroy everything.

For Ito, this is all a culturally useful part of the experience: Kids become more resilient, both practically and philosophically. "Minecraft is busted, and you're constantly fixing it," she says. "It's that home-brew aesthetic. It's kind of broken all the time. It's laggy. The kids get used to the idea that it's broken and you have to mess with it. You're not complaining to get the corporate overlord to fix it — you just have to fix it yourself." This is a useful corrective to other software. "IPhone apps are kind of at the opposite end," Ito says. "And the way that kids react when things are broken in the Apple ecosystem versus the Minecraft ecosystem is totally different. With [Apple] it's, 'Why are they broken?' Whereas with Minecraft it's like — 'Oh, they messed with something again, it's broken, we have to go figure out what they changed.' There's a sort of resignation to that the fact that you're tinkering all the time."

Because Minecraft is now seven years old, Ian Bogost will soon have students at Georgia Tech who grew up playing the game. The prospect intrigues him. "I'm very curious to see what their attitude to technology is," he says.

TWO YEARS AGO, Ava, a fifth grader who lives on Long Island, whom I met through her aunt, a friend of mine, tried Minecraft for the first time. She started a "survival" world and marveled at the jagged hills receding into the distance. But like most new players, she had no idea what to do. Night fell, mobs arrived and a skeleton staggered toward her. She mistakenly assumed it was friendly. "I was like, Oh, hi, how are you?" Ava says. "And I died after that."

Minecraft is an incredibly complex game, but it's also — at first — inscrutable. When you begin, no pop-ups explain what to do; there isn't even a "help" section. You just have to figure things out yourself. (The exceptions are the Xbox and PlayStation versions, which in December added tutorials.) This unwelcoming air contrasts with most large games these days, which tend to come with elaborate training sessions on how to move, how to aim, how to shoot. In Minecraft, nothing explains that skeletons will kill you, or that if you dig deep enough you might hit lava (which will also kill you), or even that you can craft a pickax.

This "you're on your own" ethos resulted from early financial limitations: Working alone, Persson had no budget to design tutorials. That omission turned out be an inadvertent stroke of genius, however, because it engendered a significant feature of Minecraft culture, which is that new players have to learn how to play. Minecraft, as the novelist and technology writer Robin Sloan has observed, is "a game about secret knowledge." So like many modern mysteries, it has inspired extensive information-sharing. Players excitedly pass along tips or strategies at school. They post their discoveries in forums and detail them on wikis. (The biggest one, hosted at the site Gamepedia, has nearly 5,000 articles; its entry on Minecraft's "horses," for instance, is about 3,600 words long.) Around 2011, publishers began issuing handbooks and strategy guides for the game, which became runaway best sellers; one book on redstone has outsold literary hits like "The Goldfinch," by Donna Tartt.

"In Minecraft, knowledge becomes social currency," says Michael Dezuanni, an associate professor of digital media at Queensland University of Technology in Australia. Dezuanni has studied how middle-school girls play the game, watching as they engaged in nuanced, Talmudic breakdowns of a particular creation. This is, he realized, a significant part of the game's draw: It offers many opportunities to display expertise, when you uncover a new technique or strategy and share it with peers.

The single biggest tool for learning Minecraft lore is YouTube. The site now has more than 70 million Minecraft videos, many of which are explicitly tutorial. To make a video, players use "screencasting" software (some of which is free, some not) that records what's happening on-screen while they play; they usually narrate their activity in voice-over. The problems and challenges you face in Minecraft are, as they tend to be in construction or architecture, visual and three-dimensional. This means, as many players told me, that video demonstrations have a particularly powerful explanatory force: It's easiest to learn something by seeing someone else do it. In this sense, the game points to the increasing role of video as a rhetorical tool. ("Minecraft" is the second-most-searched-for term on YouTube, after "music.")

That includes Ava on Long Island — who, after being killed by skeletons, began watching "survival mode" videos to learn how to stay alive. Soon she had mastered that, and also discovered the huge number of YouTube videos in which players review "minigames," little challenges that some Minecraft devotees design and load onto servers for others to play. (In one popular minigame, for example, players are shown a sculpture made of blocks and then try to copy it exactly in 30 seconds.) For young Minecraft fans, these videos are a staple of their media diet, crowding out TV. Ava's mother is genially baffled by this. "I don't understand it," she told her daughter when I visited them last fall. "Why are you watching other people play the game? Why don't you just play?"

Ava had recently started her own YouTube channel with her friends Aaron and Patrick, where they play and review minigames. Her father set up a high-quality microphone on a telescoping arm bolted to the computer desk; her sister drew Ava a white sign that says: "RECORDING." (Its back says: "NOT RECORDING JUST WANT YOU TO BE QUIET.") As the family's gray cat wandered around Ava's keyboard, she dialed up Patrick on a Skype video call.

When they record a video, they improvise freestyle banter while playing, and simply start all over again if something goes awry. (Which, Patrick said dryly, "happens often.") So far they have 19 subscribers and have posted 21 videos.

She played a recent video for me, in which they tried to navigate a difficult map filled with lethal, flowing lava. Their conversation is loose and funny; it's like listening to two talk-radio hosts, or perhaps the commentary over a game of basketball — if the commentary were delivered by the athletes themselves, while they play.

Considered as a genre, YouTube Minecraft videos are quite strange. They take elements of "how to" TV — a cooking show, a home-renovation show — and blend them with the vocal style of podcasting, while mixing in a dash of TV shows like "Orange County Choppers," where ingenious mechanics parade their creations.

"I don't even know that I know how to properly classify them," says Ryan Wyatt, the head of gaming content for YouTube. Minecraft videos offer a glimpse of the blurring of the line between consumers and creators. Probably two-thirds of the kids I interviewed had started their own Minecraft channels on YouTube. Most of them were happy when even a handful of friends and family watched their videos.

Some Minecraft broadcasters have become genuinely famous,

though, and earn a good living from their work. These superstars aren't children, generally; they're young adults, like Joseph Garrett, known as Stampy Cat, a 25-year-old Briton with seven million YouTube subscribers. One of my children's favorite Minecraft broadcasters is a user named Mumbo Jumbo, another Briton, whose real name is Oliver Brotherhood, known for his instructional videos on using redstone. He is 20 and began posting his videos online when he was 16, he says. At first he did it for fun, until one video — which showcases 20 complex opening-door devices — became an unexpected hit, netting him one million views. "It's not the next 'Gangnam Style,' but it was pretty good," Brotherhood says. As more fans found him, he began posting daily and now spends 50 hours a week shooting videos and replying to fans. Brotherhood delivered newspapers while in school, but a year ago his YouTube ad revenue outstripped it.

"I told my mom, 'I'm quitting my paper round,' and she said, 'Why?' And I said, 'I do a YouTube channel, and it's earning me more.'" When his mother looked at his channel, she saw it had more than 40,000 subscribers and more monthly traffic than the corporate newspaper sites she consults for.

Next year he plans to study computer science in college. "In the redstone community," he says, "a lot of people around me are programmers." Teaching himself coding is much like learning Minecraft, he found; you experiment, ask questions on Internet forums. He described his YouTube channel on his college application, and that, too, "seems to have helped," he says. The university accepted him without even seeing his final school grades.

LAST YEAR, LONDON, a 12-year-old in Washington State, set up a server so he could play Minecraft with friends. He left it public, open to anyone — which led to chaos when some strangers logged on one day to start "griefing," blowing up his and his friends' creations with TNT. He shut down the server and, a bit wiser now, started a new one with some strict rules. This one included a "whitelist," so only players preapproved by London can log in, and a plug-in — a piece of code that changes how the server works — that prevents players from destroying what others have made.

Most online games don't require kids to manage the technical aspects of how gamers interact. A hugely popular commercial game like World of Warcraft, for example, is played on a server run by its owner, Blizzard Entertainment. Game companies usually set the rules of what is and isn't allowed in their games; if you grief others, you might be banned by a corporate overlord. Or the opposite might happen: Abuse might be ignored or policed erratically.

But Minecraft is unusual because Microsoft doesn't control all the servers where players gather online. There is no single Minecraft server that everyone around the world logs onto. Sometimes kids log onto a for-profit server to play minigames; sometimes they rent a server for themselves and their friends. (Microsoft and Mojang run one such rental service.) Or sometimes they do it free at home: If you and I are in the same room and we both have tablets running Minecraft, I can invite you into my Minecraft world through Wi-Fi.

What this means is that kids are constantly negotiating what are, at heart, questions of governance. Will their world be a free-for-all, in which everyone can create and destroy everything? What happens if someone breaks the rules? Should they, like London, employ plug-ins to prevent damage, in effect using software to enforce property rights? There are now hundreds of such governance plug-ins.

Seth Frey, a postdoctoral fellow in computational social science at Dartmouth College, has studied the behavior of thousands of youths on Minecraft servers, and he argues that their interactions are, essentially, teaching civic literacy. "You've got these kids, and they're creating these worlds, and they think they're just playing a game, but they have to solve some of the hardest problems facing humanity," Frey says. "They have to solve the tragedy of the commons." What's more, they're often anonymous teenagers who, studies suggest, are almost 90 percent male (online play attracts far fewer girls and women than single-player mode). That makes them "what I like to think of as possibly the worst human beings around," Frey adds, only half-jokingly. "So this shouldn't work. And the fact that this works is astonishing."

Frey is an admirer of Elinor Ostrom, the Nobel Prize-winning political economist who analyzed the often-unexpected ways that everyday people govern themselves and manage resources. He sees a reflection of her work in Minecraft: Running a server becomes a crash course in how to compromise, balance one another's demands and resolve conflict.

Three years ago, the public library in Darien, Conn., decided to host its own Minecraft server. To play, kids must acquire a library card. More than 900 kids have signed up, according to John Blyberg, the library's assistant director for innovation and user experience. "The kids are really a community," he told me. To prevent conflict, the library installed plug-ins that give players a chunk of land in the game that only they can access, unless they explicitly allow someone else to do so. Even so, conflict arises. "I'll get a call saying, 'This is Dasher80, and someone has come in and destroyed my house,'" Blyberg says. Sometimes library administrators will step in to adjudicate the dispute. But this is increasingly rare, Blyberg says. "Generally, the self-governing takes over. I'll log in, and there'll be 10 or 15 messages, and it'll start with, 'So-and-so stole this,' and each message is more of this," he says. "And at the end, it'll be: 'It's O.K., we worked it out! Disregard this message!'"

Several parents and academics I interviewed think Minecraft servers offer children a crucial "third place" to mature, where they can gather together outside the scrutiny and authority at home and school. Kids have been using social networks like Instagram or Snapchat as a digital third place for some time, but Minecraft imposes different social demands, because kids have to figure out how to respect one another's virtual space and how to collaborate on real projects.

"We're increasingly constraining youth's ability to move through the world around them," says Barry Joseph, the associate director for digital learning at the American Museum of Natural History. Joseph is in his 40s. When he was young, he and his friends roamed the neighborhood unattended, where they learned to manage themselves socially. Today's fearful parents often restrict their children's wanderings, Joseph notes (himself included, he adds). Minecraft serves as a new free-ranging realm.

Joseph's son, Akiva, is 9, and before and after school he and his school friend Eliana will meet on a Minecraft server to talk and play. His son, Joseph says, is "at home but still getting to be with a friend using technology, going to a place where they get to use pickaxes and they get to use shovels and they get to do that kind of building. I wonder how much Minecraft is meeting that need — that need that all children have." In some respects, Minecraft can be as much social network as game.

Just as Minecraft propels kids to master Photoshop or video-editing, server life often requires kids to acquire complex technical skills. One 13-year-old girl I interviewed, Lea, was a regular on a server called Total Freedom but became annoyed that its administrators weren't clamping down on griefing. So she asked if she could become an administrator, and the owners said yes.

For a few months, Lea worked as a kind of cop on that beat. A software tool called "command spy" let her observe records of what players had done in the game; she teleported miscreants to a sort of virtual "time out" zone. She was eventually promoted to the next rank — "telnet admin," which allowed her to log directly into the server via telnet, a command-line tool often used by professionals to manage servers. Being deeply involved in the social world of Minecraft turned Lea into something rather like a professional systems administrator. "I'm supposed to take charge of anybody who's breaking the rules," she told me at the time.

Not everyone has found the online world of Minecraft so hospitable. One afternoon while visiting the offices of Mouse, a nonprofit organization in Manhattan that runs high-tech programs for kids, I spoke with Tori. She's a quiet, dry-witted 17-year-old who has been playing Minecraft for two years, mostly in single-player mode; a recent castle-building competition with her younger sister prompted some bickering after Tori won. But when she decided to try an online server one day, other players — after discovering she was a girl — spelled out "BITCH" in blocks.

She hasn't gone back. A group of friends sitting with her in the Mouse offices, all boys, shook their heads in sympathy; they've seen this behavior "everywhere," one said. I have been unable to find solid statistics on how frequently harassment happens in Minecraft. In the broader world of online games, though, there is more evidence: An academic study of online players of Halo, a shoot-'em-up game, found that women were harassed twice as often as men, and in an unscientific poll of 874 self-described online gamers, 63 percent of women reported "sex-based taunting, harassment or threats." Parents are sometimes more fretful than the players; a few told me they didn't let their daughters play online. Not all girls experience harassment in Minecraft, of course — Lea, for one, told me it has never happened to her — and it is easy to play online without disclosing your gender, age or name. In-game avatars can even be animals.

HOW LONG WILL MINECRAFT'S popularity endure? It depends very much on Microsoft's stewardship of the game. Company executives have thus far kept a reasonably light hand on the game; they have left major decisions about the game's development to Mojang and let the team remain in Sweden. But you can imagine how the game's rich grass-roots culture might fray. Microsoft could, for example, try to broaden the game's appeal by making it more user-friendly — which might attenuate its rich tradition of information-sharing among fans, who enjoy the opacity and mystery. Or a future update could tilt the game in a direction kids don't like. (The introduction of a new style of combat this spring led to lively debate on forums — some enjoyed the new layer of strategy; others thought it made Minecraft too much like a typical hack-and-slash game.) Or an altogether new game could emerge, out-Minecrafting Minecraft.

But for now, its grip is strong. And some are trying to strengthen it further by making it more accessible to lower-income children.

Mimi Ito has found that the kids who acquire real-world skills from the game — learning logic, administering servers, making YouTube channels — tend to be upper middle class. Their parents and after-school programs help them shift from playing with virtual blocks to, say, writing code. So educators have begun trying to do something similar, bringing Minecraft into the classroom to create lessons on everything from math to history. Many libraries are installing Minecraft on their computers.

One recent afternoon, I visited the Bronx Library Center, a sleek, recently renovated building in a low-income part of the borough. A librarian named Katie Fernandez had set up regular Minecraft days for youths, and I watched four boys play together on the library's server. Fernandez had given them a challenge: Erect a copy of the Arc de Triomphe in Paris in 45 minutes. Three of them began collaborating on one version; a younger boy worked on his own design. The three gently teased one another about their skills. "No, no, stop!" shouted one, when he noticed another building a foot of the Arc too wide. "Ryan, this — like this!" They debated whether command blocks would speed things up. As the 45th minute approached, they hadn't quite finished their Arc, so they gleefully stuffed the interior with TNT, detonated it and hopped onto different games.

Over in the corner, the fourth boy continued to labor away at his Arc. He told me he often stays up late playing Minecraft with friends; they have built the Statue of Liberty, 1 World Trade Center and even a copy of the very library he was sitting in. His fingers clicked in a blur as he placed angled steps, upside-down, to mimic the Arc's beveled top. He sat back to admire his work. "I haven't blinked for over — I don't know how many minutes," he said. The model was complete, and remarkably realistic.

"I'm actually pretty proud of that," he said with a smile.

CLIVE THOMPSON is a contributing writer for The New York Times Magazine and the author of "Smarter Than You Think: How Technology Is Changing Our Minds for the Better."

Closing the Gender Gap, One E-Battle at a Time

BY HAYLEY KRISCHER | JUNE 24, 2016

JUDY JETSET walked around the bar at the Playwright Irish Pub in Midtown Manhattan, checking in on the 40 people she had brought together to watch a sports event. She said hello to people she hadn't yet met, and then introduced them to others in the group. She was something of an ambassador for the assembled fans of League of Legends, a multiplayer online game that draws amateur and professional players, as well as sponsors and fantasy leagues.

Being broadcast on this Sunday afternoon in March was League of Legends' championship series. TVs around the bar showed an animated clash of mutant-like animated characters with spikes covering their arms and horns atop their heads, chasing one another through colorful mazes. The goal is to destroy the opponent's "nexus," which is an illuminated power source. When the mutants are successful, pixelated flashes of neon red, green and purple explode on a grassy battle arena in the center of the screen.

Dressed in her gold and white League of Legends custom jersey, Ms. Jetset, 29, approached a red velvet chair and introduced herself to Jenny Zhao, 18. Ms. Zhao was nestled into the cushioned seat with another friend, Amy Zhu, 21, who had urged her to attend the event.

Of the people there, a handful were women. This was a disappointment to Ms. Jetset, who works as a service desk technician at Weill Cornell Medicine in New York.

She asked Ms. Zhao what made her decide to come. She was hoping for insight to help her better promote the sport among women. "I'm not the kind of person who would just show up to an e-sports meetup," Ms. Zhao said, using the game genre's catchall term. "It makes it more comfortable that it's not a guy running this."

Ms. Jetset, in her gold and white League of Legends custom jersey, is trying to promote e-sports among women.

Games like League of Legends, which are played virtually but have created real-life communities like this one, are a new frontier in gaming, turning into a large adult-centric business in the last five years. This is how it works: People play games like League of Legends on computers or smartphones and pit themselves against other players, often strangers. Tournaments can be watched at designated times by tuning to a streaming service called Twitch.

League of Legends, according to Riot Games, the company that produces it, attracts 67 million players a month, with 27 million people playing daily.

It's unclear the exact percentage of women who are fans; Nicola Piggott, a spokeswoman for Riot, wouldn't disclose the demographic breakdown. But NewZoo, a gaming market research company, said women make up about 25 percent of the enthusiasts in the United States.

The world of gaming is male-dominated, and sexism has burdened the efforts of those who try to expand its reach. Notably there was the GamerGate scandal in which some male gamers bullied and harassed female players or others who had been designated as using video games to push a political or social agenda.

Harassment is one of the reasons Ms. Jetset uses an alias: Jetset isn't her real last name, which she declined to provide. She says the alias insulates her from being the target of online trolling. She has had male gamers comment to her on social media that she must be using League of Legends to meet guys. But most often, she is not taken seriously by some men whose interests and knowledge are no greater than hers. "The deepest sexism is the insinuation that my opinion matters less," she said.

Women like Ms. Jetset are attempting to close that fissure with smaller, more inclusive local meetups. They seek a broader outreach as well. Last year, she and another gamer, Cristina Amaya, 25, who lives in Washington and is the creator of the New York League of Legends group, founded a tournament. The Facebook group for the meetup has more than 3,000 members, and moderating the comments is a big job for Ms. Jetset and the two other gamers — both men — who oversee the page. "I've faced harassment from so many men," Ms. Amaya said. "Sexual harassment. Insulting comments. Comments about my intelligence. I wish it wasn't like that. I wish there was more I could do."

Ms. Jetset had another meetup planned for Saturday and was optimistic that it would attract a higher female turnout. "I'm always hoping more women will come, but I understand it can be very intimidating for women to come to social events geared towards gamers," she said. "All I can do is do my best to make women feel welcome."

A New Phase for World of Warcraft's Lead Designer: His Own Start-Up

BY NICK WINGFIELD | SEPT. 11, 2016

BIG VIDEO GAMES, like movies, are usually created by squadrons of people, including dozens or hundreds of artists and developers.

And yet it is an individual that often stands out for creative contributions to the most successful games. For the Mario franchise and other Nintendo hits, it is Shigeru Miyamoto. For the Grand Theft Auto series, it is Sam Houser. Within the games industry and among die-hard players, they are admired in the way Steven Spielberg and Peter Jackson are revered in Hollywood.

Rob Pardo earned a similar reputation during his 17-year career at Blizzard Entertainment, a game studio he left two years ago that has a rich legacy in the industry. Mr. Pardo was the lead designer on World of Warcraft, an online multiplayer fantasy game that came out 12 years ago and developed a following so passionate that players were willing to shell out $15 a month in subscription fees to kill orcs and goblins together.

Since its release, World of Warcraft has generated from $12 billion to $13 billion in revenue, estimates Michael Pachter, an analyst at Wedbush Securities.

"It is literally the singularly most successful game in history," said John Riccitiello, the former chief executive of Electronic Arts who now runs Unity Technologies, a game technology provider.

"There's always a lot of hands on success. I've been in the industry long enough to know that just about everybody credits him with the product," he said about Mr. Pardo.

Mr. Pardo will now have an opportunity to show whether he can translate his success inside a big company like Blizzard into a much smaller games start-up. On Monday, he plans to announce the formation of a new company, Bonfire Studios, with a handful of game veterans.

Mr. Pardo, the chief executive of Bonfire, recently raised $25 million in funding for the company from the Silicon Valley venture capital firm Andreessen Horowitz and from Riot Games, a game studio owned by the Chinese internet giant Tencent that makes League of Legends, one of the most popular online games in the world. Mr. Riccitiello and others invested in Bonfire in an earlier round.

Based in Irvine, Calif., Bonfire does not have a game in development yet. Mr. Pardo, 46, says it is safe to assume the company will make online multiplayer games, though he has not yet decided whether it will create them for mobile devices, PCs or both.

"We have a lot of confidence they're going to build something fantastic," said Brandon Beck, the chief executive and co-founder of Riot Games. "They're pretty uncompromising when it comes to quality."

For now, Mr. Pardo says he is focused entirely on hiring people to begin generating ideas and making game prototypes. Min Kim, a former executive with Nexon, an Asian game developer, and several former colleagues from Blizzard joined him as members of Bonfire's founding team. He wants Bonfire's games to recreate the social connections that many players formed when banding together in clans in World of Warcraft, a game that allows players to fraternize with one another online.

"We don't want to be constrained by genre," Mr. Pardo said. "We really want to create games that help us make those deeper connections with each other."

After leaving Blizzard, Mr. Pardo spent time designing another project, a custom home he now lives in with his family in Irvine. Allusions to geek culture are sprinkled throughout the home. There are side-by-side men's and women's bathrooms labeled Horde and Alliance after the two character factions in World of Warcraft, and wooden floors inlaid with Tetris blocks.

Mr. Pardo said his inspiration for creating a start-up with a small development team occurred while at Blizzard, during the making of Hearthstone, a digital card game that was a huge hit for the studio. At Blizzard, most game development teams were so large that some of the greatest challenges for Mr. Pardo, Blizzard's former chief creative officer, were management oriented.

The original team that created Hearthstone was unorthodox by Blizzard standards, consisting of a little over a dozen people. That relatively small size eliminated management layers that could make communication difficult and make some employees feel as if they did not have a stake in the project, Mr. Pardo said.

"Everyone got to be completely involved in game design," he said. "I feel like that team's culture was one of the strongest."

Small game studios have produced some of the most remarkable successes in the industry in recent years. During his break from Blizzard, Mr. Pardo consulted with Mr. Riccitiello at Unity — through which Mr. Pardo was able to travel the world as a kind of good-will ambassador for the company, meeting with game developers, including Supercell, the Finnish mobile games start-up that makes Clash of Clans. Tencent recently bought a controlling stake in Supercell for $8.6 billion.

Blizzard has preserved a reputation for maintaining its creative independence while being part of a larger game publisher, Activision Blizzard, which has been known to kill games in development when they fall short of its standards, rather than risk tarnishing its brand. And fans flock to Blizzard Entertainment's annual convention, BlizzCon.

"They're in many ways the Pixar of gaming, or at least the Pixar of five years ago," said Geoff Keighley, creator of the Game Awards, an Oscars-like ceremony for the industry.

"A lot of designers are typically known for one franchise," Mr. Keighley added. "The great thing about Rob is he's a bit of a polymath. He's done a lot of different styles of games at Blizzard."

Other star game designers have left big companies before and failed to match or exceed their previous success. Although there are creative challenges to working in large game companies, they do have advantages in their promotional capacity and technological tools. Mr. Pardo's supporters are not concerned.

"If you could basically draft Kevin Durant and invest in Kevin Durant as an N.B.A. player, you'd be an idiot not to," Mr. Riccitiello said.

A Non-Gamer's Guide to Fortnite, the Game That Conquered All the Screens

BY SANDRA E. GARCIA | JULY 25, 2018

FORTNITE has taken over.

Videos of people playing the game have more than two billion views on YouTube.

Drake has played it with Ninja, a celebrity among Fortnite fans. The gaming expo E3 hosted a 100-player tournament that included the rapper Vince Staples, the actor Jon Heder and the mixed martial arts fighter Demetrious Johnson.

But what, exactly, is Fortnite? If you are older than, say, 30, and not a teacher or a parent, you might have no idea. This is a guide for the perplexed.

ALL RIGHT, LAY IT ON ME.

Fortnite Battle Royale is a video game that allows as many as 100 people to meet on a virtual island and battle it out to be No. 1.

Epic Games, the creator of Fortnite, reported in June that 40 million people log on to play it each month.

It is available on every major gaming platform, including PC; Mac; consoles like Xbox One, PlayStation and Nintendo Switch; and, most recently, smartphones.

The point of the game is simple: Be the last man, woman or child standing. Kill everyone else.

It is animated in a fantasy style, more "Legend of Zelda" than "Call of Duty." The effects are not bloody or gruesome. Players can create their own characters and customize them, from what they wear to their victory dances. Accessories and appearances are very important. As in "Minecraft," there's a building element.

But make no mistake: You are there to kill. You're running out of time from the moment your feet touch the ground.

WHAT MAKES FORTNITE DIFFERENT FROM OTHER GAMES?

Unlike many high-end console games, Fortnite is free to download and play, but watch out for the in-game purchases, which can add up. According to SuperData, a video game research firm, Fortnite made $318 million in May.

Another difference from other popular multiplayer games: You can't save your progress or spawn again after your player dies.

Dead is dead.

You have to start over, making each match brand-new. Learning survival skills becomes important.

Also important: finding weapons. Your character arrives unarmed on the island via hang glider, dropping into the action.

A shrinking, bubblelike force field overhead corrals players into an ever-smaller area of the island, forcing them to move around constantly. You can't just hide and wait to ambush other players. You have to stay on the map, creating fresh opportunities for confrontations with other players that reduce everyone's chance at survival.

"In Fortnite, you don't know where everything is," said Clint Burkhardt, 29, a teacher in the Bronx. "You constantly have to watch your back, and it is never safe."

BUT WHAT OF THE CHILDREN?

For gamers, particularly those under 18 who play in teams, Fortnite became something of a social club.

Most play with a squad of friends from real life or buddies made online. In schools, the game's arrival on phones meant many distracted students before the end of the recent academic year.

"You can play with your classmates or mostly anybody around the world and maybe you can become best friends," said Jaden China, 11, of Bergenfield, N.J. They talk over their microphones in the game.

It can be addictive.

Kevin China, Jaden's father, said that during the school year he limits his son to only a couple of hours a day, or 10 to 15 hours a week.

"He is just so captivated by the game," Mr. China said. "We have to pull him off of it."

Mr. China has placed parental controls on the Xbox One he got Jaden for Christmas. He's not concerned about violence, just screen time — and accumulating in-game purchases.

In four months, Mr. China has spent $140 of real money on things like skins and victory dances for his son. "It's $20, or $25, for this or that."

When they are not themselves playing, fans of the game are watching others play. Videos of highly skilled players on YouTube and Twitch, the gaming network owned by Amazon, draw large audiences of those hoping to pick up skills and tips from more experienced gamers.

Mr. Burkhardt, who teaches students from sixth to 12th grade, said he could usually tell when a student had been up all night playing Fortnite. They would fall asleep in class.

"Sometimes when a kid does something bad," he said, "I'll suggest to the parent to take their Fortnite away."

SO, YOU'RE TELLING ME IT'S HERE TO STAY?

Perhaps. Just this month, a new season timed perfectly for the rest of the summer vacation debuted on Fortnite, bringing new challenges every week for 10 weeks, featuring historical scenarios that include Vikings, pirates and ancient Egyptians, and new tools like a cart to drive around.

So, what is Fortnite?

"It's a good game," Jaden said.

His father disagreed.

"I've tried to play it," Mr. China said, "but long have been the days since I played my Nintendo in 1989."

The old Nintendo had simple controls, he said, but the Xbox controller "has so many buttons your hand eye coordination has to be super good. It's like being in a spaceship now."

CHAPTER 2

The Fast-Paced Market for Mobile Games

While one tendency in online gaming leans toward big-budget games, an expanding app market opened another tendency: mobile gaming. These simpler games, designed for more casual play, opened a space for runaway hits that changed the video game market. Facebook games such as FarmVille, as well as hits like Candy Crush and Angry Birds, became digital empires that led traditional video game makers to take notice. Many of these games were eventually purchased by larger companies, while Nintendo developed major mobile games of its own.

Will Zynga Become the Google of Games?

BY MIGUEL HELFT | JULY 24, 2010

SAN FRANCISCO — Orientation for new employees of Zynga, the fast-growing maker of Facebook games like FarmVille and Mafia Wars, can be a heady affair given the company's outsize ambitions — all of which are embodied in Mark Pincus, Zynga's 44-year-old founder.

In a pep talk this month, Mr. Pincus told his company's newcomers that he had set out to build an enduring Internet icon, one that was synonymous with fun.

"I thought, it's 2007, and this can't be all that the Internet is meant to be," he said. There has to be more than "a garage sale, a bookstore, a search engine and a portal," he added in a good-natured putdown of the Web giants eBay, Amazon, Google and Yahoo.

And lest there be any doubt which of those giants Zynga aims to match, Mr. Pincus said the opportunity to build an online entertainment empire was "like search before Google came along."

So far, he seems on track. The Zynga Game Network, as the company is officially called, is the hottest start-up to emerge from Silicon Valley since Twitter and, before that, Facebook. Unlike Twitter, which has meager revenue, Zynga is on a path to pocket as much as $500 million in revenue this year, according to the Inside Network, which tracks Facebook apps.

While Facebook needed four and a half years to reach 100 million users, Zynga crossed that mark after just two and a half years.

JIM WILSON/THE NEW YORK TIMES

Mark Pincus, C.E.O. of Zynga, maker of FarmVille and other games, aims to build an online entertainment empire as important as Google is to search.

Zynga's empire is made up of cartoonish online games that even Mr. Pincus acknowledges are goofy. And most striking, given its financial success, is the fact that the games are free to everyone. Zynga makes money, by and large, only when a small fraction of its users pay real money for make-believe "virtual" goods that let them move up in the games or to give their friends gifts.

For instance, in FarmVille, its most popular game, players tend to virtual farms, planting and harvesting crops, and turning little plots of land into ever more sophisticated or idyllic cyberfarms. Good farmers — those who don't let crops wither — earn virtual currency they can use for things like more seed or farm animals and equipment.

But players can also buy those goods with credit cards, PayPal accounts or Facebook's new payment system, called Credits. A pink tractor, a FarmVille favorite, costs about $3.50, and fuel to power it is 60 cents. A Breton horse can be had for $4.40, and four chickens for $5.60. The sums are small, but add up quickly when multiplied by millions of users: Zynga says it has been profitable since shortly after its founding.

The company has ballooned to nearly 1,000 employees, up from 375 a year ago, and now has some 400 job openings. And investors, including Google and the Netscape founder Marc Andreessen, have put about $520 million into the company. Though some of the money was used to buy out early investors and employees, it's still a huge sum in Silicon Valley.

Zynga has been valued at more than $4.5 billion, putting Mr. Pincus, who has retained voting control over the company, on a path to become Silicon Valley's next billionaire. And, not surprisingly, Zynga has caught the attention of people beyond Silicon Valley.

At a recent gathering of media and technology moguls, Jeffrey Katzenberg, the C.E.O. of DreamWorks Animation, was asked what he would do if he were to start his career over. "I said I would like to be Mark Pincus," he recalled in an interview. "He has nailed the next killer app, the next compelling thing that's going to happen" in media.

There have been some bumps on Zynga's road to success. The games are programmed to send updates to players' Facebook friends when certain actions are completed, like planting or harvesting crops. Six million Facebook users, who grew tired of constant updates about their friends' games, joined a group called "I don't care about your farm, or your fish, or your park, or your mafia!!!"

Facebook started restricting the messages, and Zynga's traffic dropped sharply. For instance, FarmVille had a 26 percent drop, to 61 million monthly users, in July from a peak of about 83 million in March, according to AppData.com.

Mr. Pincus says he expects growth to resume with new games like FrontierVille, which a month after its release on June 9 had 20 million players. And Zynga investors say the drop in traffic had little effect on revenue because many players who dropped out didn't buy virtual goods.

Even so, some analysts and investors question Zynga's ability to keep producing hit games in an ever more crowded field. "There are only so many potential customers and only so many categories," says Rick Heitzmann, a managing director of FirstMark Capital, a venture capital firm that has invested in online game companies, though not in Zynga. "And they are burning through categories quickly," he adds, noting that Zynga already had games for pets, farms, restaurants and other subjects.

For now, however, it is hard to argue with Zynga's record.

Its games have 211 million players every month, according to AppData.com. Though that figure counts a user for each type of game he plays, it makes Zynga about four times larger than its nearest rival, Electronic Arts. Playdom is third, with 41 million users.

"I have a very high-stress life," says Alena Meeker, 32, a financial analyst at a major brokerage firm in San Francisco. "I love relaxing with the games." Ms. Meeker, who plays several of Zynga's games, says she devotes about an hour a day to them and spends $20 to $40 on virtual goods every week. She says she uses the games to connect with friends, co-workers and family.

Nathan R. Van Sleet, who lives in Oakland and is unemployed, says he plays YoVille, a game in which users create avatars and interact with others in custom-decorated homes, for up to 16 hours a day. Because he is hearing-impaired and doesn't know sign language, online forums of YoVille players have allowed him to connect with various people.

"If it were not for the forums, I would have missed the opportunity to meet these people," Mr. Van Sleet said in an e-mail.

Mr. Pincus points to these kinds of testimonials when he says that the games, while simple, have a higher purpose: connecting people. The company also donates some proceeds from virtual goods to earthquake relief in Haiti and other causes.

While some traditional developers grumble about the social-game phenomenon, which they see as a step backward in sophistication, the popularity of Zynga and some of its rivals has made the multibillion-dollar video game industry take notice. In November, Electronic Arts bought the Zynga rival Playfish for as much as $400 million. But some analysts say that most other traditional gaming companies are falling behind the trend that is taking the industry by storm.

"The only one that can catch up is Electronic Arts," says Michael Pachter, a research analyst at Wedbush Securities.

By the standards of Silicon Valley, where people like Mr. Andreessen, Mark Zuckerberg, Larry Page and Sergey Brin built Internet empires while still in their 20s, Mr. Pincus is something of an aging whiz kid.

Clad in jeans and a T-shirt, Mr. Pincus could easily blend in with Zynga's new recruits, a group of hoodie-wearing, 20-something engineers and product managers.

A serial entrepreneur, he sold his first company, Freeloader, an early Internet broadcast service, for $38 million, and took public his second, a business software maker called Support.com. He owns several homes and an airplane. Yet five years ago, around the time his third company, a social network called Tribe.net, was headed for failure, he groused in an interview that he had not yet made Silicon Valley's "A-list."

With Zynga, Mr. Pincus believes he will finally get his due. He talks of building a "digital skyscraper," a company whose services are so indispensable that someday we will look back and wonder how we managed to do without it.

As he has carved his path in Silicon Valley, he has earned a reputation as a visionary leader. Yet he is also known for his sharp elbows and irreverent style, an image he does little to dispel. He often brags about being fired from a consulting firm job for having little patience with his bosses. "I didn't believe in paying dues," he said in a public talk.

He's open about his distrust of many venture capitalists, and doesn't want to be at their mercy. "We were profitable before we raised any money," he says. "I think that gives you a better chance to sit at the table with your investors as a peer, not an employee."

He says he once barred the partners at one firm that had invested in Support.com from attending meetings "because they were not adding any value." With a touch of pride, he adds that a Silicon Valley firm turned down an investment in Zynga, telling him he was "not coachable."

Now that Zynga has shone a spotlight on Mr. Pincus as never before, his bravado has come back to haunt him. While speaking to entrepreneurs in Berkeley last year, he said: "I knew that I wanted to control my destiny. So I funded the company myself, but I did every horrible thing in the book to just get revenues right away."

Bloggers seized on those comments as an example of questionable ethics at Zynga after critics said the company was allowing deceptive advertisers into its games. Without being clear, some ads, for instance, signed up players for subscriptions to costly text-messaging services. TechCrunch, the technology blog, called the practice "Scam-Ville," and some users filed a class-action lawsuit against Zynga. The company has since filed a motion to dismiss the suit, and a hearing is expected in September.

Zynga has since pulled the ads, and Mr. Pincus now says he was misunderstood. He says he was trying to convey to would-be entrepreneurs that they needed to earn revenue quickly to gain independence from investors. "I never meant to imply you should do anything unethical," he says.

And he says he recognized that with Zynga's success, he needed to temper his attitude. "As the company has had more exposure and visibility, I have had to realize that more people take what I say seriously," he says. "I've had to grow up."

As Zynga has emerged as the most successful maker of Facebook applications, its relationship with the giant social network has become more complicated. First, there was the brouhaha over the notification system and the drop in traffic. Then Facebook said it would push all applications to use a virtual currency, Credits, on the site, and take 30 percent of proceeds. Tensions mounted, but the two companies eventually settled their differences. In May, they announced a five-year partnership expanding the use of Credits in Zynga games.

Ethan Beard, who heads Facebook's platform team, acknowledged the strains. But he said that the relationship between the two companies now was "very, very strong."

Still, some analysts predict more friction ahead, as the balance of power between the two companies shifts.

"Most people think Facebook would have been a phenomenon without games," says Mr. Pachter, the Wedbush Securities analyst. "I am not sure that's right. Twenty to 30 percent of visits to Facebook are to play games."

Zynga, which is said to be contemplating a public offering, clearly does not want to have all its eggs in the Facebook basket. It recently signed a sweeping agreement to bring its games to millions of users on Yahoo. And Mr. Pincus shared the stage with Steven P. Jobs, the Apple C.E.O., at the unveiling of the iPhone 4 to announce that FarmVille was available on the handset.

In addition, Zynga's $520 million in financing includes a recent infusion of $300 million through two, roughly equal investments from Softbank and Google, according to people briefed on the investments who spoke on condition of anonymity because they were not authorized to discuss Zynga's finances publicly. Google and Zynga are also in the early stages of exploring a collaboration, these people said. Zynga and Google declined to comment or confirm a Google investment.

When Mr. Pincus first envisioned Zynga, most investors and peers doubted that a gaming start-up could become the next big thing. But the success of games like FarmVille has silenced the critics.

"Zynga has the most revenue, growth and happy customers of any three-year-old venture we've ever backed," says John Doerr, a partner at Kleiner Perkins Caufield & Byers, the venture capital firm that has backed Amazon, Google and Netscape.

Asked how big Zynga can become, Mr. Pincus has a difficult time hiding his ambition.

"I am drinking the Kool-Aid more than anyone," he says.

From the Land of Angry Birds, a Mobile Game Maker Lifts Off

BY NICK WINGFIELD | OCT. 8, 2012

FOR A COUNTRY with a population about the size of Minnesota, Finland has produced some giant global hits in the mobile business, like the phone maker Nokia and Rovio, the company responsible for Angry Birds and Bad Piggies. A Finnish mobile games start-up called Supercell wants its crack at glory too.

The Helsinki-based company calls itself a "tablet first" games company, meaning that it designs its games to take advantage of the larger screen of the tablet rather than just blowing up smartphone games to a bigger display (though it releases versions of its games for smartphones too). For now, the dominance of Apple's iPad in the tablet market means Supercell is focused mainly on that device.

This year it introduced two games for Apple's iOS device — a farming game called Hay Day and a strategy game featuring wizards and barbarians called Clash of Clans. Both have done well, but Clash of Clans has been especially successful, occupying the No. 1 slot on Apple's top-grossing iPad game chart in over five dozen countries for weeks, according to Supercell. The games are free to download and play, but, like FarmVille and a variety of other games, Supercell sells its users in-game currency so they can speed up their game progress and buy virtual goods.

Using this model, Supercell executives say its two games are currently grossing over $500,000 a day, which translates into about $350,000 a day in revenue for Supercell after Apple takes its 30 percent cut on transactions through its iOS App Store.

Besides its country of origin, Supercell shares another similarity, an investor, with Rovio: Accel Partners, the Silicon Valley venture capital firm that was also an early investor in Facebook. The company has raised $15 million in financing from Accel, London Venture Partners and others, $12 million of it from Accel.

In a phone interview, Ilkka Paananen, the founder and chief executive of Supercell, said he did not believe that Accel's investment in Supercell was connected to the firm's investment in Rovio. He said, however, that the quality of Rovio's games had been a big influence on start-ups in the country.

"One thing they've really done for the Finnish gaming community is they've done a huge favor in raising the bar for everybody," Mr. Paananen said.

Separately on Monday, Rovio unveiled a plan to keep its Angry Birds franchise steaming forward, with a new game called Angry Birds Star Wars that it is creating in partnership with Lucasfilm.

Supercell has also opened a San Francisco office to be closer to the action in the technology industry, most notably the two big companies it works with most often, Apple and Facebook. Greg Harper, the general manager of Supercell's North America operations, said the company believed the tablet was "the ultimate game platform."

"The technology and hardware performance really is close to on-par with that of consoles," Mr. Harper said.

Supercell's executives are especially excited by the prospect of a new smaller iPad from Apple, now popularly referred to as the iPad mini. Although he was quick to say that Supercell had no inside knowledge of such a device, Mr. Harper said a smaller, less expensive iPad could help the device reach a broader audience.

Mr. Harper says he believes that the growth in the tablet market will be a bad development for dedicated portable game devices from companies like Nintendo and Sony. "That market seems in trouble to me," he said. "The iPad mini could be one of the final nails in the coffin."

Candy Crush and the Curve of Impressiveness

BY DANIEL VICTOR | MARCH 12, 2014

BACK IN 2008, I created a theory called the Guitar Hero Curve of Impressiveness. It holds that others' admiration for your gaming skills follows a bell curve: rising, rising, rising — until it crests over into a loathsome drop.

At some point, it becomes clear the time investment required by your mastery could have been better spent elsewhere. Attention shifts from your skill to the decisions that allowed you to attain that skill. Reactions change from "Wow, you're good at that" to "Wow, you do not manage your life well." And that may be right. I would likely be much better at the actual guitar had I redirected my focus in 2008 from my Nintendo to my Taylor.

The theory came back to mind a few weeks ago when I finally beat level 500 of Candy Crush, the final level, a bear of a level that required dozens of tries. I had a lot of feelings, but pride was low on the list. It felt more like closure.

But Candy Crush never leaves you alone for long. Its maker, King Digital Entertainment, regularly adds new levels and features to Candy Crush, and soon after achieving my milestone, the game maker added an additional 30 levels. I was once again bound to beating them.

It's not the first game to discover that addictive nexus between a simple game play concept and an infuriating-yet-beatable difficulty level. It's the same reason casual game players have been sucked in by titles like Angry Birds. It's easy enough to totally shut off your mind from the workday, but difficult enough to give you a genuine sense of accomplishment when you pass an obstinate level.

Candy Crush has also excelled in creating a forced scarcity, by allowing you just five lives at a time and a new one regenerating every 30 minutes. To immediately get extra lives, you can ask (read: annoy) your Facebook friends to give you some, or pay money to get your fix. That scarcity keeps the game present in your mind for longer, since it's more difficult to binge on the game for two weeks than remove it from your phone. Instead, you get a dollop at a time, forcing you to wait longer to conquer it all. (Take note, Netflix original series.)

The longer you're playing Candy Crush, the longer you're posting about it on places like Facebook and Instagram, and the longer people are seeing you play it on the train. The tactic elongates what has traditionally been the short attention span of mobile game players, which has led to the downfall of past games of obsession like FarmVille and Draw Something.

And the payoff for all the time and effort? It's life-and-work Novocaine, a dulling sensation that demands nothing of you. (Feel free to use that as your new slogan, King.) Stockholm Syndrome may even be an apt explanation.

I confess to spending most of an out-of-state bus ride on the game, wondering at the end what book I could have finished instead. Or lounging on the couch on a lazy Sunday, trying to not think about the emails I ought to be sending. Sinking so much time into a game, you can't help but wonder: What's the opportunity cost of Candy Crush? I've been neglecting my guitar again, haven't I?

I haven't otherwise been much of a gamer since the Guitar Hero days, so I'd love to hear from more serious gamers, or my fellow recent addicts: Why do we bother to reach the final level of Candy Crush, or whatever more complicated games we play on modern systems? What's the upside I'm not seeing? It's not just weakness, right?

Right?

Executive at Struggling Rovio, Maker of Angry Birds, Pushes Silver Lining

BY MARK SCOTT | SEPT. 2, 2015

STOCKHOLM — The signs are still not looking good for the maker of Angry Birds.

The woes became clear again last week when Rovio, the Finnish company that helped usher in the rise of mobile games with the Angry Birds franchise, said it would cut up to 260 jobs, or nearly 40 percent of its work force. Rovio's profit in 2014 fell roughly 70 percent compared with the year before, to just $11 million, according to regulatory filings.

Nevertheless, at a tech conference here on Wednesday, one of the company's top executives tried to strike an upbeat tone — saying the Angry Birds brand remained strong despite the financial troubles.

"We're happy with our progress, but there's room to streamline," Peter Vesterbacka, Rovio's chief marketing officer, said in an interview. "We're in a hits business, but we remain confident."

That confidence is being severely tested as the global online gaming business becomes increasingly cutthroat.

In the last couple of years, games from rivals like Supercell of Finland and King Digital of Sweden have outpaced Rovio by offering so-called freemium games. These allow people to download the online game free, and then charge users for additional services like extra lives or premium levels. The freemium business model has been particularly successful in Asian countries like South Korea, where people have become accustomed to paying for additional gaming services.

Rovio has now shifted to freemium games. Its latest offering, Angry Birds 2, has been downloaded more than 50 million times worldwide in its first month — a big number, but still behind other top games. And it may be too little, too late. While about 150 million people still play one of Rovio's games on a regular basis, the company has lost roughly 100 million monthly users from its highs.

"Freemium is really tough," Daniel Kaplan, business developer at Mojang, the maker of Minecraft that Microsoft acquired last year for $2.5 billion, said on Wednesday. "It's not hard to make games, but it's hard to get attention."

To differentiate itself from rivals, Rovio has pitched itself as more than just a gaming company. Since it began in 2009, the company has signed multiple licensing deals to spread the Angry Birds brand around the world and branched out into education and theme parks, and it will release a movie next year.

As part of its restructuring, Rovio is expected to cut back on some of those activities, though its gaming and licensing businesses remain central to its overall strategy.

"It's not very different from what Disney does," said Mr. Vesterbacka of Rovio. "Angry Birds isn't a game, a movie or a theme park. It's about the brand."

How successful Angry Birds can be in the long term, though, will depend on Rovio's ability to turn itself around, just as larger rivals like King Digital and Supercell spend more and more to publicize their online games to smartphone users.

Mr. Vesterbacka said Rovio planned to release a number of new games tied to its Angry Birds movie next year, and hinted the company may announce new brands later in 2015.

"When Rovio first came out, you could still be a small company and be successful," Niklas Zennstrom, a co-founder of Skype and investor in Rovio, said on Wednesday. "Now, you have to spend a lot on market. With games, it's very hard to get it right."

Bobby Kotick's Activision Blizzard to Buy King Digital, Maker of Candy Crush

BY MICHAEL J. DE LA MERCED AND NICK WINGFIELD | NOV. 2, 2015

ONE OF THE biggest names in traditional video games is making its boldest step yet into the fast-growing world of mobile gaming with the multibillion-dollar acquisition of a onetime darling.

Activision Blizzard said late on Monday that it planned to buy King Digital Entertainment, the home of Candy Crush Saga, for about $5.9 billion to help expand its global reach.

At a price tag of $18 a share, King will sell at a discount to the $22.50 a share that it fetched during its initial public offering last year. When the game developer went public, it was greeted with considerable enthusiasm largely on the strength of Candy Crush, where players match three or more matching candies.

King's hook was in the title's so-called freemium model, where the game was largely free to play, but additional content or virtual goodies cost real money.

But during the run-up to King's stock sale, however, the company faced questions about whether it could duplicate the success of its biggest hit, one responsible for a roughly 7,000 percent jump in annual profit.

So far, Candy Crush has remained a steady performer, ranking third in the Apple app store's top-grossing games three years after its release. But the company has said that the juggernaut has slowed down, and other games are not as popular — not even Candy Crush Soda, a related title released last year.

That lack of success in conjuring a new hit has weighed down King's profit, which fell 28 percent in its second fiscal quarter from the same time a year ago, to $119 million.

Shares in the company have fallen 30 percent below their offer price, closing on Monday at $15.54 each. (They rose 4 percent on the day, though the reason is unclear.)

Yet the declining performance of Candy Crush and other King titles did not deter Activision from a deal, according to executives from both companies. Activision saw value in King's network of players, which when combined with its own would yield an audience of more than 500 million unique users each month — bigger than Twitter's base.

The expanse of King's audience, stretching across the globe and including emerging markets that traditionally haven't spent money on expensive video game consoles and PCs, also proved attractive.

And Activision is also betting that it can figure out new ways of breathing new life into the Candy Crush franchise, much as the company has done for its own titles like Call of Duty, these people added.

Robert Kotick, Activision's chief executive, acknowledged that the deal was at a premium to where King has been trading. But he added that he believed in the long-term potential of his latest acquisition.

"They have a great franchise focus, as well as the ability to create and invent new franchises," he said in a telephone interview.

And Riccardo Zacconi, King's chief executive, added that his team would now have new opportunities by joining with Activision and its stable of games.

"We suddenly have access to the best I.P. portfolio I could ever have thought of," he said, referring to intellectual property.

Monday's deal is a departure for Activision, which has taken a cautious approaching to investing in mobile games even as rivals scrambled to sink money into the market.

Activision's best-known game franchises — Call of Duty, World of Warcraft, Skylanders and Destiny — are played on consoles and PCs, and in most cases they are sold for $30 to $60 each. It earned $835 million last year on top of $4.4 billion in sales.

"Mobile gaming is the largest and fastest-growing opportunity for interactive entertainment and we will have one of the world's most successful mobile game companies and its talented teams providing great content to new customers, in new geographies throughout the world," Mr. Kotick said in a statement.

Mobile games have grown to encompass more and more of the overall video game market. In 2015, such games are expected to generate about $14.49 billion in revenue out of about $75.41 billion in total revenue for the global games market, according to estimates by PricewaterhouseCoopers.

While mobile games have become one of the most popular categories of apps for smartphones and tablets, hits in the business can be ephemeral and the most successful publishers usually make money by charging players small fees for virtual goods and digital currency, rather than one big fee for a game.

Once-hot mobile games companies like Rovio, the maker of Angry Birds, and Zynga have struggled to adapt to shifts in taste and technology.

But there have also been some huge mobile game franchises that are still going strong. In one of the biggest acquisitions in the sector, Microsoft last year bought the Swedish developer of Minecraft for $2.5 billion, a game that is also popular on consoles and PCs.

One of Activision's biggest rivals, Electronic Arts, spent hundreds of millions of dollars on rocky acquisitions of mobile game makers like Jamdat Mobile and PopCap Games before finally hitting its stride in the business.

Activision and Mr. Kotick have taken a slower approach to the mobile gaming sector, which they have viewed as significantly different from their core business. Still, over the past year, Activision's Blizzard business came up with a huge homegrown mobile hit in Hearthstone, a digital card game.

Mr. Kotick first came to know Mr. Zacconi about three years ago when executives from King came to visit Activision's headquarters, the two men said.

The two companies stayed in touch, with Activision keeping an eye on Apax Partners, the investment firm that owns about 45 percent of King. At some point, the bigger video game maker wagered, Apax would want to sell its stake, creating a potential opportunity for a big deal.

In April, Activision approached Apax and asked what it intended to do with its stake in King according to a person briefed on the matter. That eventually led to merger discussions with the mobile-game maker, with Activision eventually signing up King's senior executives to long-term employment contracts as part of the deal. Separately, Activision reported $127 million in profit for its quarter that ended on Sept. 30, swinging from a $23 million loss the same time a year ago. Its net revenue for the period was $990 million, up 31 percent.

Pokémon Go See the World in Its Splendor

OPINION | BY AMY BUTCHER | JULY 14, 2016

IT IS STRANGE to live in a place where the skeletons of Alaskan king salmon, loosed from bald eagles' talons, sometimes plummet to the sidewalk. It is strange to live in a place where brown bears are so populous that hikers tie bells to their dogs and wrists. Where ravens as big as house cats caw and the sun barely sets into the ocean beside a dormant volcano.

Stranger still, however, to see young people hold their phones to their faces and scan this landscape for an elusive Jigglypuff.

Bubble-gum pink, more cotton candy than animal, the Jigglypuff might lurk, my students tell me, in the woods among the scattered totem poles. Or perhaps along the harbor, where yachts and trolling boats rock between rows of barnacled piers. The shells crunch beneath their feet as the kids lift their screens into the air, scanning sky and earth and sea, ignoring jellyfish and banana slugs, saying, quietly, "It's just another Rattata."

I used to be obsessed with Pokémon. A middle schooler when the game was first released in the late '90s, I beat the red version in three short days, the blue in four. I bought and ate all the candy. My companion of choice was Charmander, tiny and orange and adorable. I liked most how, like all adolescent things, he had a sweetness that quickly gave way to jutting claws, a burning tail and a glare reserved commonly for mothers.

How easily my parents bribed me in return for buying booster packs. How many weeds I pulled in pursuit of a Mewtwo. Whole rooms were vacuumed of Ritz crackers and crayon tips because of the possibility of a bumbling Snorlax, a skin-shredding Dratini.

I was, in short, enraptured. I owned three pairs of Pikachu undies and dreamed at night of Ash.

But upon the release, early this month, of Pokémon Go — the long-awaited augmented-reality iPhone and Android counterpart to the original Game Boy series — I found I had evolved to the curmudgeonly attributes of the nearly 30.

"Phones *away!*" became my mantra. I said it dozens of times a day. I was teaching at a fine arts camp in Sitka, Alaska, when the game came out — two weeks spent with talented artistic youth who had chosen to spend their summers practicing mime, ballet and photography. They were enrolled in courses in juggling, sketch comedy and opera. They were practicing the ancient Japanese pottery-making technique of raku.

But they were also playing the great Japanese time-suck of Pokémon Go, like everyone else. No longer was I enraptured. The game seemed an incredible nuisance in the classroom, but also in the cafeteria and the auditorium, at our nightly events and on the campus green. The students pointed their cameras at the blackboard, bouncing digital Poké Balls to capture creatures, laughing when a wormy Weedle landed on another student or slithered across a desk. They were respectful when class started, or when the lights dimmed for a performance, but still I resented the game and its viral international reception.

More than anything, I couldn't understand why my students — living in pristine, picturesque Alaska — were so enamored of the invented wilderness superimposed on their screens. The real thing was all around them.

But these were primarily Alaskan students. They represented 45 Alaskan communities, several of them Native, many of them isolated, and banana slugs were not of interest.

Days later, upon return to my Ohio home, when I no longer felt I had to set an example, I downloaded the game myself.

My community came to life in vibrant shades of pastel blue and green, the grid of my neighborhood alive with magic. I caught a Bulbasaur on my comforter. A fluffy Eevee lurked within the garden. In jest, my boyfriend and I walked a block in pursuit of rustling leaves that indicated an animal not yet captured in our Pokédex. We caught him and walked the block. Then another. We walked five miles.

I moved to my suburban Ohio neighborhood two months ago, and have lived in the state for less than two years, after relocating from the East Coast. I drive to work and I come home. The restaurants I most frequently patronize are a mile away at most. My daily life occurs within a radius of 10 to 20 miles, and much of that is countryside, yellow or green but always empty.

Adventure, then, means a life outside Ohio — its many casseroles and flea markets, all those churches and ice-cream shops. It means, more generally, the world outside the United States.

But wandering my neighborhood, progressing downtown toward Poké Stops — blue diamonds scattered among communities that revitalize your avatar's supplies — my world became suddenly foreign. I noticed everything. I stood on Sandusky Street, the town's main drag, amassing Poké Balls, and read from a small blue bubble that on this site, 153 years ago, residents formed the Fifth United States Colored Troops. Four were later awarded congressional Medals of Honor.

"Did you know that?" my boyfriend asked. Then, minutes later, "Did you know that? Or that?"

We weren't the only ones doing this. The neighborhood buzzed with people out exploring, an enormous uptick for a Monday evening. The whole idea of Pokémon Go is to visit where you have not been, to trace sites both new and foreign. A local Creole restaurant became a Poké Stop, unlocked only from within, and so people clustered within the lobby, waiting for tables or ordering takeout. Next to City Hall, a high school couple laughed as they caught a growling Nidoran. A man in a Slipknot T-shirt flashed his phone at me, saying, "Do you believe these Pidgeys?"

The game thrives most through collaboration. A block away, the century-old cinema glowed pink from a "lure module" another player had set, and a crowd of us shared stories until its 30 minutes of magic had dissipated.

Certainly there is the argument — already frequent, predictable and boisterous — that it is a particular brand of tragedy that leads an entire generation of American children into the great outdoors while clutching phones before their faces.

Still, fads fade. Pokémon Go will no doubt go out of style. But I'll still feel more tethered to my community and aware of all it offers — I'll know that the Creole restaurant is indeed very good, and that the movie theater is rather charming, and that this place of dairy and agriculture is not Alaska but is no less lovely.

In the meantime, it seems far from terrible to see a father and son racing down suburban sidewalks. To spend an evening not sitting passively before a TV, but interacting simultaneously with both our media and the world. To share in an experience, however seductive or silly, that forces us to go out and explore together.

The sun was nearly down when, for the first time in my two years here, my boyfriend and I drove out to the state park in pursuit of a water creature. I caught him, big and blue with a golden shell, at the bank of a lake, and then we put our phones away, peeled down to our bathing suits, and waded into Ohio's green water, forgetting altogether what it was that brought us there.

AMY BUTCHER, an assistant professor of English at Ohio Wesleyan University, is the author of the memoir "Visiting Hours."

Mario, Nintendo's Mustachioed Gaming Legend, Arrives on iPhones

BY NICK WINGFIELD AND VINDU GOEL | DEC. 14, 2016

SEATTLE — What happens when one of the best-selling games in history comes to the most popular category of electronic devices in the world? A mustachioed plumber in overalls is about to reveal the answer.

On Thursday, after nearly a decade of doing its best to ignore the explosive growth of smartphones and tablets, Nintendo is finally bringing a game based on its beloved character Mario to mobile devices.

People have been able to play Mario games on portable devices made by Nintendo since the early 1980s, but the release of the new Super Mario Run represents the first time Nintendo has put out an installment for devices made by another company — in this case, iPhones and iPads from Apple.

It is a watershed moment for a game character who is as recognizable to many as Mickey Mouse. Mario is widely estimated to be the best-selling game franchise ever, with more than a half-billion copies sold since the plumber first showed up in the game Donkey Kong in 1981. So iconic is the character that Shinzo Abe, the prime minister of Japan, appeared at the closing ceremony of the Summer Olympics in Rio de Janeiro this year dressed as Mario to promote the next Summer Games in Japan.

Releasing Mario on phones and tablets was once an unthinkable move for a quirky company that had for years insisted that making both game software and the hardware it ran on was essential to its magic.

Nintendo finally relented as general-purpose mobile devices increasingly cut into sales of its portable game players. Other games publishers filled the void on mobile devices left by Nintendo, threatening to erode the relevance of its game properties, including Zelda and Donkey Kong, for a new generation of players.

"They've really let their brand wilt the last few years," said David Cole, a games analyst with DFC Intelligence. "But I think we've seen how strong that brand still is. There is potential to bring it back."

Nintendo made some curious choices with Super Mario Run that suggest it is not yet entirely comfortable with mobile devices. The game will require a constant internet connection, which could make it difficult to play on airplanes, in subways and in other areas where connections are unreliable or nonexistent. Company executives have said in interviews that Nintendo is requiring an internet connection, in part, to prevent piracy of the game.

"We remain confident that the play style means that the game can be played in a wide range of locations and situations," Kit Ellis, a Nintendo spokesman, said in an emailed statement.

Nintendo is also pricing the game in an unconventional way for the mobile market. While it will allow players to sample portions of Super Mario Run for free, Nintendo will charge $9.99 for full access to the game. A vast majority of mobile games are free, but some provide players with opportunities to pay $1 or more for useful items inside a game or for access to new challenges.

Only a few mobile games — Minecraft is one notable example — have successfully charged as much as Nintendo plans to, analysts said.

"Ten bucks for the mobile environment is really high," said Joost van Dreunen, chief executive of SuperData Research, a firm that tracks the games market. "That's a tough ticket."

Still, it is hard to understate the passion players feel for Nintendo games, sustained by an almost bottomless well of nostalgia for the company's products from the 1980s and 1990s. Earlier this month, a $60 miniature version of an old Nintendo console, called the NES Classic Edition, sold out in stores within minutes of going on sale. Nintendo-themed areas are coming to Universal theme parks in Japan, Hollywood and Orlando, Fla.

This summer, Pokémon Go, a mobile game based on an entertainment property partly owned by Nintendo, was an enormous hit. That game, created by an independent company called Niantic, benefited from the fact that it was free to play. It also made innovative use of a technology called augmented reality, awarding points to players for capturing Pokémon characters that they found in public locations through their smartphone cameras.

Mitch Lasky, a venture capitalist with Benchmark and a longtime investor in games companies, said the success of Pokémon Go shows how much pent-up demand there is for Nintendo properties on devices made by other companies. He also said he was encouraged that Shigeru Miyamoto, the renowned Nintendo game designer who created Mario and other Nintendo classics, had a hand in Super Mario Run.

"I think Mr. Miyamoto is the greatest game designer of his generation, and his apparent involvement on Run gives it a ton of credibility," Mr. Lasky said.

The game has also benefited from months of promotion by Apple. Just before Apple unveiled the iPhone 7 in September, Timothy D. Cook, Apple's chief executive, announced Super Mario Run and invited Mr. Miyamoto to show it off on stage. The company has heavily promoted the game in its app store since then, with a banner at the top urging fans to sign up to be notified the moment it is available to be downloaded. As of mid-October, 20 million people had done so, according to Apple, which declined to release a more current figure.

Last week, Apple began offering visitors to its retail stores a sneak peek at the game, with a playable demonstration version loaded onto the iPhones and iPads on display. Mr. Miyamoto also sat for an interview in front of a packed house at Apple's store in the SoHo neighborhood of Manhattan.

"This is unprecedented marketing support from Apple," said Randy Nelson, the head of mobile insights at Sensor Tower, a mobile analytics firm. He predicted Super Mario Run would be "in terms of downloads, the largest app launch in history."

With so many new games arriving on mobile phones, keeping players engaged is always a challenge. Even Pokémon Go faded after the initial hype. According to App Annie, a mobile analytics firm, 23 million Americans played it at least once in November, down from 66 million in July.

Do not expect Nintendo to stop making its own game players anytime soon. The company recently revealed plans to begin selling a new console, Switch, in March that can be played both on televisions in the home and on the go. Analysts believe Nintendo's primary focus will be on its own devices rather than on mobile games.

"It's probably more of a sideshow in their overall strategy," said Mr. van Dreunen of SuperData Research. "I don't think Nintendo is getting out of the hardware game."

HISAKO UENO contributed reporting from Tokyo.

How I Became Addicted to Online Word Games

BY LIESL SCHILLINGER | MARCH 18, 2017

EVERYONE HAS HEARD grim tales of lives blighted by online gaming, stories that sound like urban legends even when they actually happened. There is the friend of a friend who played Second Life so obsessively that his real-life business failed; the web addict in Taiwan who died after a three-day binge; or even Alec Baldwin, kicked off a plane after refusing to stop playing Words With Friends. But most of us have too much sense to let online games mess up our travel plans, much less hook us on what the Chinese call "digital heroin," right?

Well, I used to think so.

At a weekend share house not long ago, I found that the virtual-reality virus had infected me, and I'm beginning to suspect the condition is endemic. Like a 2-year-old who tries to widen a picture in a storybook with her fingers, I have grown confused about the difference between page and screen.

This revelation came after a friend spotted a battered Boggle box on a shelf in the rental house and asked me to join her in a round. I hadn't played the physical, letter-dice-and-egg-timer version of the game in a decade, but in my teens I had been a Boggle demon, the terror of my high-school word nerd crowd. Afraid I would demoralize my friend if I unleashed my full word-seeking powers, I resolved to lose the first game. And then she flipped the timer, and I looked down at the letters on the tray, and despaired. I saw F-E-E-N and F-E-A-N; F-E-A-Z-E, F-A-N-T and F-E-N-T; S-P-E-E-R and E-T-H-S.

Were they real words? I had no idea. I had played them countless times in Words With Friends, but couldn't remember which ones had scored points and which had been rejected, or what any of them meant, if anything. Unlike the tabletop games Boggle and Scrabble, Words With Friends has no penalty for guessing.

In the past, I loved word games because I loved words. The vocabulary I brought to them had accreted organically, from books I read — "wizening" from D. H. Lawrence; "ayah" from Frances Hodgson Burnett; "crewelwork" from Jane Austen. But the words I absorbed in online games had lodged themselves in my neural map without definitions or context. At the weekend house, as my friend blithely jotted down D-R-A-G and P-E-A-R and S-P-E-A-R, I came to a standstill. I no longer knew what was a real word and what wasn't.

This was particularly vexing because I had perceived this danger nearly a decade ago, and thought I had dodged it. In 2008, a television critic and fellow word lover had urged me to engage with her on a word game app called Prolific. At first, I demurred, messaging back that I had tried another app, Scrabulous, and hadn't liked it; too much like Scrabble (a game I've always found frustrating because letter-luck plays too big a part).

Prolific was different, she fired back. It was just like Boggle. You logged on any time of day or night, joined a round with a friend or with strangers across the globe; then a letter grid popped up, and all of you raced to find words in the same grid in the same three-minute span. Charily I messaged her back: "I'll give it a go."

At the time, the weather was glacial and I was housebound, felled by a severe cold. Dizzy with DayQuil, unable to focus on work, I logged into Prolific and played my first round, foolishly confident that my lengthy word list would loft me into the winners' circle. Then the scores came up. I had been trounced, routed, utterly crushed, by a legion of far-flung opponents — and above all by a man I'll call Balthazar Tong, who had whomped me by hundreds of points, and beaten the others, too.

The victors had listed all the words I had found, and a Jackson Pollock-splatter of letter bursts that looked like no words I'd ever seen: aas, coit and deme; elt, haka and reh; sena, slae and soop. My ranking after that game was something like 60,000th in the world — out of 60,001, I believe. Sneezing and furious, I vowed to defeat them all. Especially Balthazar Tong.

For the next few weeks, racked by coughs but unwilling to leave my desk even for a glass of water, I played one game after another — until 11 p.m., 1 a.m., 2 a.m., then 4 — breaking only for DayQuil, then NyQuil. As hours and days slid by, my cold increased in violence, a mountain of tissues piled up in my study and my Prolific status rose.

Soon I started keeping an alphabetized list of words that worked and words that didn't, typing them up and making printouts, reducing the font so all of the words would fit on one page, for speedy glimpsing during each lightning round. After every game, I would grab a Magic Marker and scribble in new words that had popped up, type them into my list, then print again. When my cold turned into bronchitis, I interrupted play to go to the doctor and pick up Zithromax, then rushed back to 24/7 keyboard combat.

A neighbor, hearing of my illness, stopped by with chicken soup and oranges. Observing the trash heap of tissues on my desk and floor, the sheaves of rumpled printouts beside my keyboard, scrawled with addendums in rainbow colors, she grabbed my wrists. "Liesl," she said. "This looks like something out of 'A Beautiful Mind.' " As she spoke, my eyes darted helplessly to the waiting onscreen grid. My ranking was now in the top 1,000. If my friend would only leave, I reasoned, I might be able to break into the top 500 by dawn. But she lingered. "You need an intervention," she said. Nodding with feigned contrition, I wheezed out a long, dry cough and promised to put Prolific aside and take a nap. Once she left, I began again.

A few days later, I had a fever of 101, and was nearing Prolific's Olympus. I still was losing to Mr. Tong, but now I was beating my other boogeymen: Drasko Spitz, Phuong Soh and Minerva Nelson. When I joined a game with Leander Fishkin, and he unjoined it as soon as my name appeared in the roster, I rejoiced. I then joined a game with my original Prolific pusher, the TV critic, who still saw the game as "fun." Afterward she messaged back that she would never play with me again. My bronchitis was on the verge of turning into pneumonia, but I was powerless to stop playing.

There was only one way to break the spell, and providentially, it occurred in time to keep me out of the emergency room. The Prolific king-of-kings, Balthazar Tong, joined a round with me. Somehow, I beat him. Flights of doves, cymbals clanging, inexpressible feelings of relief. I was free. In the next half-hour, I canceled my Prolific account, threw away my word printouts and booked a flight to Miami, hoping to recover my health and reason on the beach, with a pile of novels. I never played Prolific again. I accepted that I was a Prolifoholic.

When, after a couple of years, I started playing Words With Friends, I dared it only because I didn't even like the game. Like Scrabble, it bugs me because if you get worse letters than your rivals, you can't win.

Over time, though, my Words With Friends habit mounted, incrementally, until it became normal for me to have six or seven games going at once at all times. (This is still the case.) I didn't notice when legions of nonsense constructs marched through the portcullis of my psyche and overran my internal dictionary.

It was not until the emergence of the Boggle game at the share house that I realized I hadn't kicked the online word game addiction after all. If Prolific had been my heroin, Words With Friends was my methadone. I had become a cautionary tale — a gaming addict no better than the rest.

Tens of millions of people play Words With Friends, and millions of others play the Boggle-clone apps that have arisen in the wake of Prolific, like Wordtwist, Word Crack, Wordruggle and Wordament. For most players, it's probably harmless, innocent diversion.

Yet I can't help worrying about the long-term effects of the epidemic of tainted wordplay that has spread across the world in the past decade. I wonder if memorizing gibberish will damage everyone's ability to communicate; if cheating with language will erode the certainties of spelling; and if I'll ever be able to play a clean game of Boggle again. But most of all, I wonder what has become of Balthazar Tong.

LIESL SCHILLINGER is a New York–based critic, translator and moderator.

An Angry Birds Empire: Games, Toys, Movies and Now an I.P.O.

BY CHAD BRAY | SEPT. 5, 2017

LONDON — The digital world is littered with one-hit wonders — companies that tried to turn a single successful brand into a big-time business only to be eclipsed by changing technology and consumer tastes.

Zynga, which once paraded sheep in Times Square to celebrate a spinoff of its highly addictive FarmVille, is worth far less than it was when it went public in 2011. King Digital Entertainment tried to build an entire Candy Crush empire, but sold out to a traditional game maker two years ago.

The maker of Angry Birds, Rovio Entertainment, hopes to defy that trend.

Rovio found success in a smartphone game that pitted a brightly colored feathered flock against an army of green pigs, spawning a series of sequels, a line of toys and clothing, and a feature film. Now, the Finnish company is planning an initial public offering that could value the company at roughly $2 billion, in a test of whether investors will find favor in a single franchise and whether the business can evolve.

Rovio helped usher in the rise of smartphone games, building a juggernaut around the Angry Birds brand. In the game, released in 2009, users fling birds at elaborate structures built by pigs that have stolen their eggs.

The game's idiosyncratic concept now has several spinoffs that rank among the most downloaded apps on smartphones and tablets. Rovio's titles have been downloaded 3.7 billion times, the company said.

"The Angry Birds Movie" grossed around $350 million worldwide. A sequel is planned for release in September 2019.

Rovio has ridden the wave of a rapidly expanding mobile gaming market. The industry's worldwide revenue was about $16 billion in 2012 and is forecast to top more than $50 billion this year, according to data from SuperData Research, a data provider on the games industry.

But Rovio now needs to prove it can profit beyond the success of Angry Birds. Its games business, which includes the original Angry Birds and more than a dozen spinoff titles, accounted for 79 percent of its revenue in the 12 months through June.

"They need to find a way to diversify their brand portfolio in the future," said Atte Riikola, a research analyst at Inderes in Helsinki, Finland. "They have had problems in their history when trying to diversify, so it won't be an easy task to do."

The company has done a good job creating offshoots of its flagship game, like Bad Piggies and Angry Birds Match. The company has also introduced several non-Angry Birds titles in recent years, including a puzzle game called Fruit Nibblers and a game tied to the pop singer Shakira.

"The hardest part in the app market is to find the users, to get people to download your game," said Tero Kuittinen, chief strategist at Kuuhubb, a Finnish company focused on lifestyle and mobile video game applications. "If you have a well-known intellectual property — you have something that is instantly recognizable, James Bond, 'The Wizard of Oz,' any kind of property like that — it helps you a lot. Why wouldn't they leverage Angry Birds?"

But it is still unclear whether Rovio has the framework or model to fuel innovation and expand beyond its main brand. The mobile gaming environment is especially competitive.

"At a certain stage, you will need a formula for more efficient innovation success," said Mark DiMassimo, the chief executive and chief creative officer at the advertising agency DiMassimo Goldstein. "You're going to need to get to winners faster than other folks, more efficiently than other folks. If you don't, you're going to be on the losing end of the category."

The announcement of the public offering marks a turnaround for Rovio, which struggled financially in the years after the initial release of Angry Birds. The company, which started out by selling its games, was caught flat-footed as consumers gravitated to games offered through a so-called freemium model, in which players download the game for free and pay for additional features. Rovio has since switched from paid apps to free downloads of its games.

Mikael Hed, a co-founder, stepped down as its chief executive in 2014, and the company announced plans to cut nearly 40 percent of its work force the next year. (Mr. Hed is still executive chairman of Rovio Animation, which helped bring "The Angry Birds Movie" to the big screen last year.)

Rovio returned to a profit in 2016 and reported revenue of 191.7 million euros, or about $228 million, last year.

Rovio is the latest game maker to turn to the public markets after becoming a cultural phenomenon, following in the footsteps of Zynga and King Digital.

Zynga, the company behind not only FarmVille but also Words With Friends, was valued at $7 billion when it went public in 2011. Its shares are now trading at a third of the initial price.

The company rose to fame with social games played on Facebook, but it was slow to recognize the move to mobile gaming. While it has since shifted its focus, the company has not been able to repeat its earlier success.

King Digital, the Swedish maker of Candy Crush, went public in 2014, but was sold for about $5.9 billion a year later to Activision Blizzard. It sold at a discount to its initial listing price as it struggled to replicate the success of its biggest hit.

The founder of Supercell, a Finnish rival behind the hit Clash of Clans, opted not to pursue an initial public offering, instead selling a 51 percent stake to the Japanese telecommunications giant SoftBank in 2013 for about $1.5 billion. Last year, the Chinese internet giant Tencent paid $8.6 billion for a controlling stake in Supercell.

Rovio said that the aim of the initial public offering was to help it carry out a growth strategy, and that it would use its shares for possible acquisitions and rewards to its employees.

Rovio said the initial public offering would consist of the sale of stock by its main shareholder, Trema International Holdings, and other shareholders. The company is also seeking to issue additional shares worth €30 million, or about $36 million, in the offering.

"That's really the question for the market around this I.P.O.: To what extent do we believe the company can exploit its existing intellectual property, and to what extent can it go again and deliver another big hit?" said Will McInnes, the chief marketing officer at Brandwatch, which monitors social media trends.

China Embraces a Game About a Traveling Frog

BY KAROLINE KAN AND AUSTIN RAMZY | JAN. 26, 2018

BEIJING — A few short weeks after its release, a Japanese mobile game featuring a traveling frog has become a hit in China.

Why, exactly, is a bit hard to explain.

The game is called Tabi Kaeru, or Travel Frog. It was created by Hit-Point, the Japanese company that released the popular game Neko Atsume, or Kitty Collector, in 2014.

It is played like this: A frog sits in its stone hut, eating and reading, while you collect clover from the front yard. The clover is used to buy food, which the frog takes on a journey.

Once the frog leaves on a trip, it's unclear how long it will be gone. Sometimes it travels for hours or even days. When it returns, it provides snapshots and mementos of its journey.

If the 1980s arcade game Frogger is frog travel as sheer terror on the open road, Travel Frog is more like waking up at your destination after a restful nap.

For whatever reason, this seems to be a concept that Chinese mobile gamers have been waiting for. The state-run Xinhua news agency reported on Tuesday that Travel Frog had risen to the top of the free simulation game category in Apple's App Store in China. It is being widely discussed on social media, where users post photos of their frogs' adventures.

The secret of the game's appeal isn't readily obvious. But the frog is cute, for one thing. Some players say they enjoy the feeling of traveling vicariously.

And it's also really easy.

"You don't need to do a lot of things, you don't even need to think about anything," said Yu Ting, a 28-year-old accountant in the northeastern city of Tianjin. "It's not a competitive game, so it's very relaxing."

The game also has a strong connection to child rearing. Before the frog leaves on a trip, you have to pack its lunch. And in Chinese, the word for "frog," wa, is a homophone for a word for "baby."

"My friends and I all call the frogs our 'frog sons,' " said Gao Lang, 22, a graduate student in Beijing. "After raising this frog, I suddenly understand the feeling of being a parent, at least partly. And I think when I am traveling somewhere far in the future, I will try to send some photos to my parents."

On Thursday came a sign that Travel Frog had truly made it: finger-wagging from the People's Daily, the official newspaper of the Communist Party of China, which warned people not to embrace the ethos of the game.

"Live to the fullest and don't be just a lonely 'frog-raising youth,' " it said Thursday on its official Weibo account.

To most players, that probably doesn't need saying.

"Some people compare it with raising a child," said Zhu Juan, 35, a sales director at a medical instrument company in Beijing. "I have a 3-year-old daughter, and I know it's different."

KAROLINE KAN reported from Beijing, and **AUSTIN RAMZY** from Hong Kong.

Esports and Gaming as Public Spectacle

As video games rose in popularity, their attraction began to include watching the most skilled players and dynamic personalities. Beginning in countries like South Korea, gaming became esports, and people filled stadiums by the thousands to watch their favorite players. Though the United States was slower to professionalize competitive gaming, American esports soon became a legitimate force. With it came the rise of "streaming," where players broadcast their playing on YouTube and Twitch, highlighting their playing and their personality, and making fortunes in the process.

The Land of the Video Geek

BY SETH SCHIESEL | OCT. 8, 2006

SEOUL, SOUTH KOREA — At first glance, the sprawling COEX mall here seems like any other urban shopping destination. On a late-summer Thursday, there were the bustling stores and lively restaurants, couples on dates and colleagues mingling after work.

But then there were the screams.

Frantic, piercing, the shrieks echoed down the corridors from one corner of the vast underground complex. There hundreds of young people, mostly women and girls, waved signs and sang slogans as they swirled in the glare of klieg lights. It was the kind of fan frenzy that anywhere else would be reserved for rockers or movie legends.

ESPORTS AND GAMING AS PUBLIC SPECTACLE **113**

Or sports stars. In fact the objects of the throng's adoration were a dozen of the nation's most famous athletes, South Korea's Derek Jeters and Peyton Mannings. But their sport is something almost unimaginable in the United States. These were professional video gamers, idolized for their mastery of the science-fiction strategy game StarCraft.

With a panel of commentators at their side, protected from the throbbing crowd by a glass wall, players like Lim Yo-Hwan, Lee Yoon Yeol and Suh Ji Hoon lounged in logo-spangled track suits and oozed the laconic bravado of athletes the world over.

And they were not even competing. They were gathered for the bracket selection for a coming tournament season on MBC Game, one of the country's two full-time video game television networks. And while audiences watched eagerly at home, fans lucky enough to be there in person waved hand-lettered signs like "Go for it, Kang Min" and "The winner will be Yo-Hwan {oheart}."

All in all it was a typical night in South Korea, a country of almost 50 million people and home to the world's most advanced video game culture: Where more than 20,000 public PC gaming rooms, or "bangs," attract more than a million people a day. Where competitive gaming is one of the top televised sports. Where some parents actually encourage their children to play as a release from unrelenting academic pressure. Where the federal Ministry of Culture and Tourism has established a game development institute, and where not having heard of StarCraft is like not having heard of the Dallas Cowboys. The finals of top StarCraft tournaments are held in stadiums, with tens of thousands of fans in attendance.

Noh Yun Ji, a cheerful 25-year-old student in a denim skirt, had come to the COEX with 10 other members of one of the many Park Yong Wook fan clubs. "I like his style," she said of Mr. Park, who plays the advanced alien species called Protoss in StarCraft. "I watch basketball sometimes, but StarCraft is more fun. It's more thrilling, more exciting."

South Korea's roughly $5 billion annual game market comes to about $100 per resident, more than three times what Americans spend. As video games become more popular and sophisticated, Korea may provide a glimpse of where the rest of the world's popular culture is headed.

"Too often I hear people say 'South Korea' and 'emerging market' in the same sentence," said Rich Wickham, the global head of Microsoft's Windows games business. "When it comes to gaming, Korea is the developed market, and it's the rest of the world that's playing catch-up. When you look at gaming around the world, Korea is the leader in many ways. It just occupies a different place in the culture there than anywhere else."

Just after one Friday night, Nam Hwa-Jung, 22, and Kim Myung-Ki, 25, were on a date in Seoul's hip Sinchon neighborhood. At a fourth-floor gaming room above a bar and beneath a restaurant specializing in beef, the couple sat side by side on a love seat by the soda machines, each tapping away at a personal computer. Ms. Nam was trying to master the rhythm of a dance game called Audition, while Mr. Kim was locked in a fierce battle in StarCraft.

"Of course we come to PC bangs, like everyone else," Mr. Kim said, barely looking up. "Here we can play together and with friends. Why would I want to play alone at home?"

A few yards away, amid a faint haze of cigarette smoke, five buddies raced in a driving game called Kart Rider while two young men nearby killed winged demons in the fantasy game Lineage. Another couple lounged in a love seat across the room, the young man playing World of Warcraft while his date tried her skills at online basketball.

Ms. Nam glanced up from her screen. "In Korea, going and playing games at the PC bang together is like going to a bar or going to the movies," she said.

South Korea is one of the most wired societies in the world. According to the Organization for Economic Cooperation and Development, Korea had 25.4 broadband subscriptions per 100 residents at the end of last year. Only Iceland, with 26.7, ranked higher; the United States had only 16.8.

Yet despite the near-ubiquity of broadband at home, Koreans still flock to PC bangs to get their game on. There is a saying in Seoul that most Koreans would rather skip a meal than eat by themselves. When it comes to games it seems that many Koreans would rather put down the mouse and keyboard than play alone.

Woo Jong-Sik is president of the Korea Game Development and Promotion Institute. Speaking in his office far above Seoul, in the towering Technomart office and shopping complex, he explained the phenomenon simply: "For us, playing with and against other people is much more interesting than just playing alone against a computer."

It started out that way in the United States too. But as game arcades with their big, clunky machines started disappearing in the 1980's, gamers retreated from the public arena and into their homes and offices. In the West gaming is now often considered antisocial.

There are certainly concerns about gaming in South Korea. The government runs small treatment programs for gaming addicts, and there are reports every few years of young men keeling over and dying after playing for days on end. But on the whole, gaming is regarded as good, clean fun.

In Seoul's dense Shinlim district, Huh Hyeong Chan, a 42-year-old math tutor, seemed to be the respected senior citizen at the Intercool PC bang, which covers two floors, smoking and nonsmoking.

"Among people in their 20's and 30's I think there is no one who hasn't been to a PC bang because it's become a main trend in our society," he said from his prime seat at the head of a row of computers. "Most people think it's good for your mental health and it's a good way to get rid of stress. If you exercise your brain and your mind in addition to your body, that's healthy."

And cheap. At most PC bangs an ergonomic chair, powerful computer and fast Internet link cost no more than $1.50 an hour.

Lee Chung Gi, owner of the Intercool bang, said: "It's impossible for students in any country to study all the time, so they are looking for interesting things to do together. In America they have lots of fields and grass and outdoor space. They have lots of room to play soccer and baseball and other sports. We don't have that here. Here, there are very few places for young people to go and very little for them to do, so they found PC games, and it's their way to spend time together and relax."

Top pro gamers in South Korea don't get much chance to relax. Just ask Lim Yo-Hwan. Mr. Lim, 27, is the nation's most famous gamer, which makes him one of the nation's most famous people.

"Normally our wake-up hours are 10 a.m., but these days we can sleep in until around 11:30 or noon," he said at the SK Telecom StarCraft team's well-guarded training house in Seoul. "After we wake up we have our breakfast, and then we play matches from 1 p.m. until 5. At 5 p.m. we have our lunch, and then at 5:30 for an hour and a half I go to my gym, where I work out. Then I come home and play until 1 a.m. After 1 I can play more matches or I can go to sleep if I want."

He smiled. "But not many players sleep at 1."

Mr. Lim sat in what might be called the players' lounge: a spacious parlor of plush couches and flat-screen televisions. In an adjoining apartment, the focus was on work. More than a half-dozen other members of the team sat at rows of PC's demolishing one another at StarCraft, made by Blizzard Entertainment of Irvine, Calif. Outside, guards for the apartment complex kept an eye out for overzealous fans.

"Without covering myself up in disguise it's really difficult to go out in public," Mr. Lim said. "Because of the Internet penetration and with so many cameras around, I don't have privacy in my personal life. Anything I do will be on camera and will be spread throughout the Internet, and anything I say will be exaggerated and posted on many sites."

"It's hard because I can't maintain my relationships with friends," he added. "In terms of dating, the relationships just don't work out. So personally there are losses, but I don't regret it because it was my choice to become a pro gamer."

Hoon Ju, 33, the team's coach and a former graduate student in sports psychology, added: "Actually when he goes out we know exactly where he is at all times. That's because the fans are constantly taking pictures with their cellphones and posting them to the Internet in real time."

Mr. Woo of the federal game institute estimated that 10 million South Koreans regularly follow eSports, as they are known here, and said that some fan clubs of top gamers have 700,000 members or more. "These fan clubs are actually bigger in size than the fan clubs of actors and singers in Korea," he said. "The total number of people who go spectate pro basketball, baseball and soccer put together is the same as the number of people who go watch pro game leagues."

The celebrity of South Korea's top gamers is carefully managed by game-TV pioneers like Hyong Jun Hwang, general manager of Ongamenet, one of the country's full-time game networks. "We realized that one of the things that keeps people coming back to television are the characters, the recurring personalities that the viewer gets to know and identify with, or maybe they begin to dislike," he said. "In other words, television needs stars. So we set out to make the top players into stars, promoting them and so on. And we also do a lot of education with the players, explaining that they have to try to look good, that they have to be ready for interviews."

For his part Mr. Lim cultivates a relatively low-key image. He knows that at 27 he is nearing the end of his window as an elite player. There are 11 pro teams in the country, he said, and they are full of young guns looking to take him down. But he said experience could make up for a few milliseconds of lost reflexes.

"The faster you think, the faster you can move," he said. "And the faster you move, the more time you have to think. It does matter in that your finger movements can slow down as you age. But that's why I try harder and I work on the flexibility of my fingers more than other players."

Despite the stardom of pro gamers, in most Korean families it's all about school. That is a big reason the game market in South Korea is dominated by personal computers rather than by game consoles like Sony's PlayStation and Microsoft's Xbox that are so popular in the United States and Europe. (The deep historical animosity Koreans feel toward Japan, home of Sony and Nintendo, is another reason.)

"In Korea it's all study, study, study, learn, learn, learn," said Park Youngmok, Blizzard's Korean communications director. "That's the whole culture here. And so you can't go buy a game console because all it is is an expensive toy; all it does is play games. But a PC is seen here as a dream machine, a learning machine. You can use it to study, do research. And if someone in the household ends up playing games on it" — he paused, shrugged and grinned — "that's life."

Cho Nam Hyun, a high school senior in a middle-class suburb south of Seoul, knows all about it. During his summer "vacation" he was in school from 8 a.m. until 8 p.m. (During the school year he doesn't finish classes until 10 p.m.) On his desk in his family's impeccable apartment sits a flip chart showing the number of days until his all-important university entrance exams.

But no matter how hard he studies, Mr. Cho tries to get in just a little gaming, and with his parents' encouragement. "They are at school all the time, and then they have additional study classes," said his mother, Kim Eun Kyung, "so games are the best way to get rid of their stress."

His father, Cho Duck Koo, a photographer, added: "Certainly the games can be a distraction, and now that he is studying for the university exam he plays much less, but in general gaming helps the children with strategic thinking and to learn to multitask. We've told him if he goes to university we will get him the best PC possible."

It's all part of a dynamic that has taken technologies first developed in the West — personal computers, the Internet, online games like StarCraft — and melded them into a culture as different from the United States as Korean pajeon are from American pancakes.

Sitting outside another packed soundstage at another cavernous mall, where around 1,000 eSports fans were screaming for their favorite StarCraft players over the Quiet Riot hard-rock anthem "Cum On Feel the Noize," a pinstriped banker illustrated how South Korea has become the paragon of gaming culture.

"We're not just the sponsors of this league," Kim Byung Kyu, a senior manager at Shinhan Bank, one of the country's largest, said proudly. "We're the hosts of this league. So we have a bank account called Star League Mania, and you can get V.I.P. seating at the league finals if you've opened an account."

"When I'm in the U.S., I don't see games in public," he added. "The U.S. doesn't have PC bangs. They don't have game television channels. What you see here with hundreds of people cheering is just a small part of what is going on with games in Korea. At this very moment hundreds of thousands of people are playing games at PC bangs. It's become a mainstream, public part of our culture, and I don't see that yet in the U.S. In this regard, perhaps the United States will follow and Korea will be the model."

Video Gaming on the Pro Tour, for Glory but Little Gold

BY RICHARD NIEVA | NOV. 28, 2012

WHEN SEAN PLOTT was 15, he and his older brother, Nick, begged their mother to fly them from Kansas to Los Angeles for a video game tournament.

For Cara LaForge, their single mother, who was struggling to start a new business, the expense was steep. Her sons passionately insisted they could win, so she conceded. But there was a catch: "If you don't win, you're going to pay me back," she recalled.

They didn't win.

Ms. LaForge didn't make her sons pay her back, but in a way, they have. Eleven years later, she is the business manager at Sean Plott's company Day[9]TV, which broadcasts daily videos online geared toward gamers. The two brothers are celebrity personalities in the world of StarCraft II, a popular strategic game. Sean Plott was featured on Forbes's 30 under 30 list in 2011.

Video games have evolved from an eight-bit hobby to a $24 billion industry in 2011, according to the NPD Group, a research firm. As more people play games, more of them compete in structured competitive tournaments, complete with fans, sponsors and lucrative contracts. It's a long and tough slog, as Ms. LaForge's story suggests.

But just how crazy is it to encourage your gamers to get off the couch and hit the road to play for money? Maybe a little crazier than encouraging a child to become a professional bowler or chess master. Professional gamers follow a track similar to professional golfers, entering several tournaments a year and collecting prize money, said Brian Balsbaugh, founder of the eSports Management Group, an agency that serves pro gamers. (Yes, professional gaming has already advanced to the point where the top players have agents.) Major League Gaming — the scene's largest tournament organizer in North

America — hosts four major competitions a year. In November, it held the Fall Championship in Dallas.

Although some players are paid handsomely — the top prize in Starcraft II tournaments in North America is $25,000, and corporate sponsorships can pull in much more cash — for most, the prospect of making good money as a pro is still doubtful. Professional gaming's financial structure is top-heavy, so only the best players earn significant incomes of $100,000 to $200,000. "We're at a point where only about 40 people in the U.S. can make a living playing video games," said Sundance DiGiovanni, chief executive of Major League Gaming. "I'd like to get it to a hundred. I think we're a year or two away from that."

For a beginner, expenses like travel, hotels and registration fees can be costly, especially for a parent picking up the bill for a teenager with little income. Tom Taylor, who goes by Tsquared and is a champion at the shooter game Halo, recalled selling things like PlayStation games or Pokémon cards on eBay to pay his way.

To cover those costs, talented players can sign contracts to play for sponsored teams, like Mr. Taylor's squad, Str8 Rippin. The average salary for competitive gamers ranges from about $12,000 to $30,000, said Marcus Graham, a former pro and gaming personality who is also known as djWHEAT.

These players make the biggest commitments, playing about eight hours a day. Some sponsors have the players live together to build chemistry with teammates. Mr. Taylor, who ran team houses in Chicago and Orlando, Fla, said the practice time jumps to 10 to 14 hours a day as a tournament approaches.

A well-known team franchise like Evil Geniuses — considered the Yankees of pro gaming — can dole out lucrative contracts, over six figures for superstar players, said Alexander Garfield, the team's chief executive.

The most marketable stars — those with a mix of talent and charisma like Mr. Taylor and Kelly Kelley, a k a MrsViolence — can attract

The Taipei Assassins won the League of Legends championship in October at the Galen Center in Los Angeles.

individual sponsorships independent of a team. SteelSeries, a maker of gaming accessories, signs deals for up to $80,000 that cover major expenses for the most prominent gamers, said Kim Rom, the company's chief marketing officer. SteelSeries also makes smaller deals with relative unknowns it thinks have potential. The company sponsors up to 200 gamers in the United States, though only about 20 pros get those top-notch deals, Mr. Rom said.

But while professional gaming is increasingly popular, in recent years the gaming world has had to rework its marketing approach. Organizers have sought to rebuild the scene since 2008, when a few leagues, like the Championship Gaming Series, folded. Before 2009, mainstream broadcasters like ESPN2 featured tournaments on television. Since then, the league has turned to the Web, rather than TV, for its lifeblood. This year, Major League Gaming began broadcasting on GameSpot.com, a division of CBS Interactive. That change in direction is an example of altered expectations — at least in the short term — for the kinds of careers professionals will have. It is also a warning that the odds of making it big are slim. Ken Yamauchi, the father of Coby Yamauchi, a 16-year-old professional and one of the scene's rising stars, said he always reminded young gamers, "Use this as a steppingstone. You expect to support a family, buy a house through gaming? It's not going to happen."

The smartest personalities build their brands enough to make the bulk of their money on peripheral jobs. The Plott brothers are popular eSports broadcasters, providing live commentary during matches. Many gamers also have sponsored YouTube channels and sign contracts with services like Twitch.tv, a Web site that streams tournament video. Morgan Romine, a former captain of the all-female team Frag Dolls, now works full time as an eSports liaison for Red 5 Studios, a video game maker based in California.

If the tournaments aren't a way to make money for college, one's experiences on the competitive circuit can look good on college applications.

"Colleges want to see kids who are passionate in one area," said Bev Taylor, founder of the Ivy Coach, a college admissions consultancy. But she suggests framing it in a way that emphasizes the community aspect of gaming. "They won't accept anyone they think will just sit in their dorm room all day," she said.

Once a player is accepted into college, gaming can still have its perks. Mona Zhang founded the Collegiate StarLeague while she was a freshman at Princeton, organizing intercollegiate tournaments for StarCraft II players. The league now has over 600 teams from schools like Yale and the Massachusetts Institute of Technology. The league also gives out two "Excellence in eSports" scholarships, said Ms. Zhang, who has since graduated.

Competitive gaming even has its fingerprints on the corporate world. In 2011, Sean Plott helped start the After Hours Gaming

League, a gaming tournament that pits teams from technology companies like Google, Twitter and Facebook against each other.

Mr. Plott describes it as "a modern twist to the corporate softball league." It's not going to make anyone rich, but it's fun. As video games were designed to be.

Seeking to Be Both N.F.L. and ESPN of Video Gaming

BY ALAN FEUER | AUG. 9, 2013

THE MUST-SEE MATCH this month on Major League Gaming, North America's foremost video-gaming league, was the long-awaited face-off between FaZe and Impact, two of the world's top teams at the military shooting game Call of Duty: Black Ops II.

FaZe, still smarting from falling short in a match last spring in Dallas, had rearranged its lineup and was hoping its brand-new captain, Replays, could keep in check Impact's sharpest shooter, an accomplished slayer on the submachine gun who goes by the name Killa.

It was shortly after 7 on a Thursday night, and the four-person teams — their members scattered across eight cities from Las Vegas to Philadelphia — had already logged on to their Xbox consoles. They now stood ready to do battle in a digital competition broadcast live on the Internet, to thousands of fans, from the league's main studio on the East Side of Manhattan.

"Hey, guys, and welcome to M.L.G. Pro Scrims!" Chris Puckett, the league's celebrated host, exclaimed as the camera lights clicked on and a jib-boom angled toward him for a close-up.

Sitting at his broadcast desk, Mr. Puckett, using a microphone and headset, turned to face his color commentator, the retired gamer RevaN (John Boble).

"So, Rev," Mr. Puckett went on, in a dramatic SportsCenter voice, "we've got a heck of a match tonight. FaZe versus Impact. Who goes home a winner?"

If you are not part of the target demographic — young men, 18 to 34 years old — you probably have never heard of Major League Gaming and are no doubt unaware that in the last 10 years, it has gradually emerged as the N.F.L. of the professional gaming world. M.L.G., as the league is often called, has played a central role in turning video

John Boble, at left, a retired gamer, and Chris Puckett during a match broadcast.

games, once considered mere entertainments, into an organized, and highly lucrative, form of sport.

Through its live-streamed matches and arena shows, the league has put to rest that antiquated image from the days of the arcade — the slacker playing Pac-Man with quarters in his pocket — and has helped to replace it with the professional "cyber-athlete," the full-time gamer who can earn six figures and supplement his income with public appearances and product endorsements from companies like Intel or Red Bull.

Since its start in 2002, M.L.G.'s Web site has hosted millions of viewers who log on in the evening to watch its competitions and then click on to YouTube in the morning to catch the latest highlight reels of matches they missed. Two months ago, a crowd of 20,000 packed into the Anaheim Convention Center in Southern California for the league's Spring Championships, a three-day contest that unfolded — in the real world — in an atmosphere more commonly reserved for basketball or football. There were thunder sticks and screaming fans and vendors selling soft drinks. There were T-shirts, hoodies and other merchandise at the concession stands.

"It was just like any traditional sport — except they were playing video games," said Sundance DiGiovanni, M.L.G.'s co-founder and chief executive officer. "We've always said there would come a time when parents would tell their kids, 'Hey, get back inside and practice your video games. You're going to have to pay for college someday.' "

That time could be coming sooner than you think. According to the market research firm DFC Intelligence, the global video-game industry is poised to have revenues this year of $66 billion, up from $63 billion in 2012. As the largest "e-sports" organization in North America, Major League Gaming has experienced a similar trend in growth. About 8 million people — mostly men and mostly in their 20s — are registered as users on its Web site, majorleaguegaming.com. In the last three years, the number of unique viewers visiting the site in a year has rocketed to 11.7 million from 1.8 million — an increase of more than 500 percent.

The Web site, a slickly packaged portal covered with videos and the league's official logo (a white controller on a field of red, white and blue), is the entry point for professional gamers and amateurs alike. While teams like FaZe and Impact play on the site in cutthroat competitions broadcast live to 170 countries, hundreds of thousands of casual players also use it every month — for a basic fee of $10 — and compete against their peers.

"One thing that M.L.G. has done quite well is to foster a layer of amateur players, almost like a farm league," said T. L. Taylor, an associate professor at M.I.T. and the author of "Raising the Stakes: E-Sports and the Professionalization of Computer Gaming."

"It's another way that they've signaled their connection to athleticism," Professor Taylor said. "They've tried, intentionally, to link themselves to the conventions of sport."

Among those who have finally come around to the idea that Call of Duty — or StarCraft II — is indeed a sport are United States immigration officials, who just last month classified the world's top video-game players as professional athletes. Under lobbying from M.L.G. and its partners in the industry, the government decided it would issue athletes' visas to certain gamers from abroad, allowing them to visit the United States more easily for tournaments.

The federal ruling was based on a gaming metric known as APMs, or actions per minute. In StarCraft, for example, a military strategy game, the average player can generally reach about 70 APMs. The world's most accomplished gamers — like the celebrated BoxeR, who lives in South Korea — can execute as many as 400. That means BoxeR, a master of the game, is able to perform more than six separate keystrokes or movements of the mouse every second.

"The dexterity and visual acuity that takes is just incredible," Mike Sepso, M.L.G.'s co-founder and president, said. "When people say it doesn't take athletic prowess, I tell them they should try it. Ordinary people just can't do what professional gamers do. They have an agility that even Michael Jordan didn't have."

Major League Gaming was born by chance in the late 1990s at a party at the Chelsea Hotel. Mr. Sepso and Mr. DiGiovanni, both then in their 20s and unknown to each other, were invited by a mutual friend.

"I remember walking in," Mr. Sepso, 41, recalled recently, "and seeing this guy with an irritating mustache and an earring, ignoring everyone and playing Gran Turismo."

Mr. DiGiovanni, 40, remembered the meeting this way: "Some guy in a bad blue motorcycle jacket challenged me to play. I thought, 'Why not? I'll play him. If he dresses like that, how good could he be?' "

Within an hour a friendship had been formed, and within another year or two, the men had started a business, Gotham Broadband, which helped develop business plans and market strategies for telecom concerns.

Mr. Sepso, who attended Babson College in Wellesley, Mass., and Mr. DiGiovanni, who studied film at the Tisch School of the Arts at N.Y.U., were among that early class of techies who made a profit in the city's first Internet boom. Near the turn of the millennium, however, they sensed that the bubble was about to burst and sold their company, escaping into exile to live off their earnings and play video games. Late one night, they found themselves at a bar and, wearied by the scene, decided to go home and play Xbox. A handful of acquaintances went with them — stockbrokers, barflies and their girlfriends.

"It was a bunch of late 20s, A-type, New York personalities sitting in a room, competing over video games," Mr. Sepso said. "Sundance and I had the same thought. If we're here doing this, then there have to be others who are out there doing it, too."

Within months, they had persuaded the owner of a Chinatown nightclub, Fun, to let them project video games on a wall above the dance floor for spectators to watch; eventually they developed an underground following in the local gaming world.

This was at a moment when Mr. DiGiovanni started hearing rumors about secret gaming tournaments held on college campuses around the country. He and Mr. Sepso hit the road, visiting these tournaments on a kind of learning tour. "They were totally unorganized," Mr. DiGiovanni said. "And we had some money left from our first business, but it was quickly running out. So I told Mike, 'If we're really going to do this, let's do it now.'"

Major League Gaming was established that same year, and for its first four seasons it was kept afloat exclusively through financing from its founders. Then, in 2006, Oak Investment Partners, a local venture capital firm, gave the pair money, and by 2012 it had invested nearly $60 million in the league. While Mr. Sepso refused recently to discuss the company's revenues, he said that this year would be its best in terms of total earnings. "It's the first full year that we'll be profitable," he said.

As with any digital concern, M.L.G.'s worry from the start was how to make money from its growing traffic on the Internet. Seventy percent of its revenue comes from advertising, Mr. Sepso said. As might be expected, from the beginning, game developers, both large and small, bought advertising on the site. But in a testament to the league's core audience — boys with wealthy parents and their own disposable income — mainstream entities like carmakers, soft-drink companies and the United States Army started to arrive.

Advertisers have also been enticed by a certain buzz that surrounds the league. Mr. Sepso scored a coup in June, at the tournament in Anaheim, when he convinced a group of N.B.A. stars to appear at the event in a special "All-Star Showdown." Among those who attended was Dwight Howard, then of the Los Angeles Lakers, a gamer sufficiently committed to the sport that he showed up in the middle of his free-agency negotiations — arguably the most important moment of his career.

"But the best part is that our hard-core fans ran right by him and tried to get to Nadeshot," Mr. Sepso said, referring to a hugely popular gamer who plays for OpTic, a team based in Chicago, and who has more than 200,000 followers on Twitter and nearly a half-million subscribers to his YouTube channel.

Mr. Puckett, the 27-year-old on-air host, has also become a bold-face name. He often signs so many autographs at tournaments that his Sharpie runs dry.

Mirroring the ambitions of the industry as a whole, M.L.G.'s next step is to try to break out of the video-gaming ghetto and attract a wider audience. Starting this month, the league will gradually unveil an eclectic, five-hour block of evening Internet broadcasts, adding lifestyle shows to its already popular live-streamed competitions.

Heading up this effort is Mr. Puckett, who has added the title of vice president for programming to his portfolio. The ideas he has kicked around include a John Madden-like show on trash-talking gamers, and reality-television-style documentaries on professional gaming houses — residential compounds where top teams live and practice together around the clock.

For the last five years, M.L.G., in a partnership with Dr Pepper, has produced the gaming world's version of a home-makeover show, "The Dr Pepper Ultimate Gaming House," in which lucky contestants have

Employees at M.L.G. at the league's offices at 34th Street and Park Avenue.

their shabby home-gaming systems overhauled with state-of-the-art consoles and 56-inch television sets.

"We want to approach things like a cable network and program prime time from at least 7 to 11 every weeknight," Mr. Sepso said. In other words, M.L.G. is no longer content to simply be the N.F.L. of professional gaming, but wants to be its ESPN and HGTV, too.

"My goal," Mr. Puckett said the other day, "is to take these guys who already have a following, enhance their production values and put them on the network."

In a few weeks, the league expects to announce a wide-ranging partnership with an undisclosed film and television studio to develop projects and to further integrate celebrity personalities into its broadcasts. "Basically, it's a major strategic relationship to spearhead our plans to move M.L.G. aggressively into mainstream culture," Mr. Sepso said.

As for Mr. Puckett, his main objective is to create professional gaming's equivalent of ESPN's SportsCenter, a daily digest of gaming news, competition highlights, and game and product reviews. He envisions a program broken into 8 or 10 three-minute segments that could, as he put it, "bridge the hard-core gaming community to the casual viewer and still keep everyone entertained."

In the meantime, though, he continues to announce matches for "M.L.G. Pro Scrims," and by the third game of the Best of 11 series between FaZe and Impact, Impact was dominating the field, led by Killa, who had racked up 36 kills, 10 captures and 4 defends.

"There's just no doubt about it, Killa is the best Hardpoint Call of Duty player out there today," Mr. Puckett's partner, RevaN, said. "He's fantastic on the submachine gun. He makes the kills happen."

The match went on with a stream of commentary that sounded familiar in its rhythms, if not its details — "Nice snipe there by Slacked!" "Ooh, Killa with the knife kill on Spacely!" — and each game came to a conclusion with the Round-Ending Killcam, which replayed particularly skillful moves in slow motion.

At one point the broadcast paused for a commercial break. Mr. Puckett, grinning at the camera, made a comment that applied not just to the match at hand, but also to M.L.G.'s future.

"Don't go too far, guys," he insisted. "We'll be back."

What's Twitch? Gamers Know, and Amazon Is Spending $1 Billion on It

BY NICK WINGFIELD | AUG. 25, 2014

THE VIDEO IN video games is suddenly a billion-dollar business.

Video games have long been something people played. But in the last few years, thanks in part to fast Internet access and multiplayer games, the games have become something that people sit back and watch, too. On Monday, that new habit enticed the web giant Amazon to reach a $1.1 billion deal to buy Twitch, the most popular website for watching people play games.

The deal for Twitch is the latest sign of the way forms of behavior once seemingly on the fringe can, in the hands of tech entrepreneurs, turn into huge online communities in no time. Twitch did not exist a little over three years ago, and it now has 55 million unique viewers a month globally, helping turn games into a spectator event as much as a participatory activity.

Those millions of eyeballs are valuable to web companies, and Amazon, although usually known for its retailing, is no exception. To win in its bid for Twitch, Amazon had to outmaneuver a who's who of the tech world, including Google — strongly suggesting that these companies think the era of video-game viewing is just starting. It also underscored Amazon's growing appetite for controlling and delivering content to digital devices, especially the tablets and smartphones made by Amazon.

"Broadcasting and watching gameplay is a global phenomenon," Jeff Bezos, the chief executive of Amazon, said in a statement, "and Twitch has built a platform that brings together tens of millions of people who watch billions of minutes of games each month."

Twitch specializes in live videos of people playing games, including regular Joes blasting away in Call of Duty, a popular shooting game, and elite players who earn million-dollar payouts at professional game tournaments. Twitch viewers typically see the screen of a broadcaster, featuring the game being played, along with a video feed of the player's face and a chat window so they can communicate with the player and others watching the action.

The site has attracted enough viewers to put it among 15 most-trafficked websites around the world, according to data compiled by Sandvine, an Internet networking company. Twitch viewers flock to the site to improve their gaming skills by watching people who have mastered a game or just to get a closer look at games before buying them. Some of the biggest followings on Twitch are of people who are simply amusing, rather than the best players.

Gamers can transmit games over Twitch by using PCs along with consoles like the PlayStation 4 and Xbox One. Twitch says that people watch more than 16 billion minutes of its videos each month. More than 1.1 million unique broadcasters use Twitch to stream video.

The company shares advertising revenue with people who broadcast over its service. While the audiences for many broadcasters are so small they make little money, some broadcasters are said to earn over six figures a year.

The service has dovetailed with the rise of e-sports, as professional gaming is often called. Twitch broadcasts the action from live tournaments for big games like League of Legends and Dota 2. Professional gamers also use Twitch to let spectators watch their practices, inviting them to ask questions about playing techniques.

"Before Twitch, gaming was something you did in the basement in the glow of your monitor," said David Cowan, a venture capitalist with Bessemer Venture Partners, a big investor in Twitch. "Now it's something you can do in groups with hundreds and thousands of people."

It is not clear exactly how Amazon intends to fit Twitch into its eclectic and ever-expanding portfolio of businesses. It could help accelerate the company's advertising ambitions by giving it a huge video network to pump commercials through. This year, Amazon ad revenue is expected to jump 40 percent, to over $1 billion, according to estimates from eMarketer, a technology research firm.

Amazon plans to let Twitch operate independently, out of its offices in San Francisco, according to Emmett Shear, Twitch's chief executive. The deal includes stock Amazon is paying to retain Twitch employees and $970 million in cash, said a person briefed on the terms of the deal.

For months, Amazon has been in a nasty public feud with the Hachette Book Group over the pricing of that publisher's e-books, showing just how important unfettered access to digital content is to the company's ambitions. Amazon has started to invest heavily in developing original television shows and movies, and even to develop games of its own, all of them accessible to a growing array of devices, including an Amazon smartphone, television set-top box and tablets.

"We're heavily invested in games already," Mike Frazzini, vice president for Amazon games, said in an interview. "We have a healthy business selling games to customers."

James McQuivey, an analyst at Forrester Research, said the Hachette dispute had shown that Amazon needed to invest more in content that it can control. "It puts them into a vulnerable position where they need to make sure they have hours and hours of stuff to pump into these devices," Mr. McQuivey said.

But Amazon could also face pricing disputes with game publishers, since Twitch has agreements with major game makers that allow it to broadcast content from their games.

Some publishers, though, are interested in more lucrative deals with Twitch than the ones they have now. One such publisher, Activision Blizzard, which owns the games Hearthstone and Call of Duty, is unlikely to continue its current business arrangement with Twitch, according to a person briefed on the company's thinking, who spoke on the condition of anonymity because the discussions were private.

Twitch "loves Blizzard's games," Mr. Shear said, and the company wants to help Blizzard make more money from the site.

"It's a huge marketing value for them," he said.

Mr. Shear said that the site also provided a community meeting place — recalling an old ritual, when gamers would crowd one another in arcades.

"What Twitch supports isn't even new — it's old," he said. "But what's new, that showed up in the past few years, is the entire online community can participate en masse in this kind of full interactive experience."

MIKE ISAAC contributed reporting.

Activision Buys Major League Gaming to Broaden Role in E-Sports

BY NICK WINGFIELD | JAN. 4, 2016

ACTIVISION BLIZZARD, the publisher of Call of Duty and other hit video game franchises, has acquired the assets of Major League Gaming, an early organizer of professional video game competitions.

The deal, worth $46 million, is relatively small for a company the size of Activision, which has a market value of over $27 billion. But it could play a significant role in Activision's broader ambitions to become a bigger player in the media business.

Robert A. Kotick, chief executive of Activision Blizzard, said he saw an opportunity to build a bigger mainstream audience for e-sports through more professionally produced events modeled on traditional athletic competitions and the broadcasts that bring them into homes.

While most of its e-sports events are more likely to be watched over the Internet, as most professional e-sports competitions are today, Activision intends to bring them to viewers through a traditional television channel distributed by cable and satellite providers, Mr. Kotick said.

"I have a simple vision for this," Mr. Kotick said in a phone interview. "I want to build the ESPN of video games."

Activision is buying Major League Gaming largely for its online broadcasting network, MLG.tv, which streams game matches to consoles, personal computers and mobile devices. Late last year, Activision, based in Santa Monica, Calif., announced the formation of Activision Blizzard Media Networks, a division focused on the growth in e-sports.

Activision has already begun bringing in people with extensive backgrounds in broadcasting and e-sports. In October, Activision hired Steve Bornstein, the former chief executive of ESPN and NFL Network, to run its new media division. It also hired Mike Sepso, a co-founder of Major League Gaming, to serve as a senior vice president of the division.

As part of the acquisition, Sundance DiGiovanni, the other co-founder of Major League Gaming and its chief executive, will join Activision.

Major League Gaming, founded 12 years ago, will continue to organize professional video game competitions featuring games made by Activision and other publishers.

Other big publishers have begun increasing their investments in e-sports in recent months. In December, Electronic Arts, the publisher of the Madden and Battlefield franchises, formed an e-sports division and appointed Peter Moore, its former chief operating officer, to run it. Last year, Microsoft increased its investments in a professional tournament for players of Halo, its science-fiction shooter game.

But no publisher has been more successful at fostering a large e-sports audience than Riot Games, whose October championship match for its arena battle game, League of Legends, was viewed by as many as 14 million people at one time, up from 11 million the prior year.

For the most part, publishers like Riot have viewed e-sports as a way to energize their fan bases by showcasing the talents of the most highly skilled players. The competitions are not generally big sources of profits on their own but benefit publishers indirectly by improving sales and increasing the online purchases that occur within games.

Mr. Kotick, of Activision, said that he saw similar benefits for his company's games, but that he believed organized competitions would become a big business in their own right, as corporate sponsors and advertisers become more familiar with the category.

Activision is hardly the first company to consider the broadcasting of e-sports competitions as a crucial piece of the e-sports business. Twitch became a streaming powerhouse by allowing professionals and amateurs to broadcast matches, and it was eventually acquired by Amazon for nearly $1 billion. YouTube, which is owned by Google, has also turned itself into a popular destination to view gaming videos of all kinds.

Much of the gaming content on Twitch and YouTube is contributed by users, though these platforms also broadcast professional competitions. Mr. Kotick thinks an e-sports network singularly focused on premium content — including slickly produced competitions and news shows akin to "SportsCenter," on ESPN — will be able to attract more interest from advertisers.

"We think user-generated-content networks are great and widely available," he said. "This is really focused on premium content."

The studios within Activision that make its games will be able to decide whether to team with Activision's own broadcasting arm to air their competitions or an outside company, Mr. Kotick said.

In addition to Call of Duty, the digital card game Hearthstone, developed by the Blizzard side of the company, has developed a sizable e-sports following. Blizzard's StarCraft helped create the modern e-sports scene, which first emerged in South Korea over a decade ago.

Esports Sees Profit in Attracting Female Gamers

BY GREGORY SCHMIDT | DEC. 21, 2016

MARK RELIGIOSO, a brand manager for the video game publisher Bandai Namco Entertainment, wants more women to be involved in the professional gaming arena known as esports, where players compete in video game tournaments to win thousands of dollars in prize money.

So this year, Mr. Religioso began planning "Bonnie and Clyde" tournaments, where esports teams consist of one man and one woman. He also began laying the groundwork for a mentoring program to foster interest in esports among women.

"These are baby steps so that we can get more women on the team," he said. "We need to make the scene a welcoming place."

Mr. Religioso's efforts are one of several recent moves by video game makers and publishers to increase diversity in esports, which is rapidly becoming one of the video game industry's most visible segments. As more women play video games, the esports industry is starting to focus on getting more of them involved in professional competition to help the effort expand and become mainstream.

Revenue from esports is expected to surpass $1 billion worldwide by 2018, yet the viewership for esports is only 15 percent female, according to the market research firm SuperData. There is little data on the number of women who actually play esports, but anecdotal evidence suggests the figure may be small.

Efforts to increase diversity in esports go back more than a decade but have started gathering momentum. In 2003, the French esports company Oxent began organizing annual women-only tournaments; 40 teams competed in the 2016 tournament in Paris, an increase of 25 percent over the previous year.

Twitch, the Amazon-owned site that livestreams video game play, began hosting Misscliks, a support community for women in gaming,

Diane Tran at her computer, training for video game competition.

three years ago after some of its founders became dismayed by the lack of women in esports. Twitch also established Inclusivity City, an area for diversity organizations, at its annual convention, TwitchCon, which ran Sept. 30 to Oct. 2 in San Diego.

And this year, apart from Bandai Namco's efforts, Intel and the esports company ESL partnered to form AnyKey, an advocacy organization that seeks to create support networks and provide opportunities for women in esports.

Many women gamers welcome these efforts. With a predominance of professional male players, the culture of the video game industry has long been perceived as misogynistic. Women in esports have frequently faced heckling from teammates and anonymous threats of rape and murder.

"It's an extremely toxic environment for women," said Stephanie Harvey, 30, who is a top competitor in esports tournaments for the game Counter-Strike: Global Offensive. "To be a woman in esports, you have to have a thick skin."

How effective these efforts will be in drawing more women to esports is uncertain. Although Oxent, which has run the Electronic Sports World Convention for 13 years, has organized women-only tournaments for years for Counter-Strike, there is little evidence that they are encouraging more women to play competitively. Some gamers think the events reinforce the idea that women are not capable of competing with men.

Lâm Hua, the head of content at Oxent, said the women-only tournaments were not entirely successful in drawing more women to esports, but after much debate, the company decided that they were "the first step in the grand scheme of women recognition in the sport." For now, he said, they were "a necessary evil."

Other diversity efforts in esports have focused on normalizing the idea of women in gaming. Anna Prosser Robinson, a programming manager and onscreen personality at Twitch, helped push the company's diversity initiatives after seeing women rise up, then drop out of esports.

"We would see these awesome, compelling women be excited" about esports, she said. "Six months later, they would be gone." The goal of Misscliks, she said, was to provide support and resources to encourage those women to create a network on Twitch and stay in esports.

Ms. Prosser Robinson also helped bring diversity to TwitchCon this year with Inclusivity City, a physical space on the convention floor that hosted several diversity organizations like AnyKey and Hack Harassment, as well as a Smash Sisters tournament for women who play Nintendo's Super Smash Bros. fighting games.

"Inclusivity is a core value of our brand," Chase, a Twitch spokesman who goes by one name, said of the diversity effort at the convention. "It was a success this year and definitely something we could consider for next year."

AnyKey, the creation of Intel and ESL to increase the number of women in esports, focuses on two areas. One is research and discussion of the diversity issue, headed by T. L. Taylor, a professor at the Massachusetts Institute of Technology, and the other is initiatives and solutions, led by Morgan Romine, a former esports player.

AnyKey organized a women-only esports tournament in March at one of the industry's largest events, the Intel Extreme Masters competition in Katowice, Poland. Ms. Romine said she saw women-only tournaments as a way to strengthen players' skills and move them into open competition.

"There is a lot of work that needs to be done, giving more women confidence and experience in that space," she said.

Mr. Religioso of Bandai Namco said he began noticing the lack of female esports players at regional esports tournaments last spring, like Final Round in Atlanta and Combo Breaker in Chicago.

With the growth in esports, he saw an opportunity to reinvigorate interest in the company's Tekken franchise. Next year, Bandai Namco will release Tekken 7, a one-on-one fighting game that the company

Coach Erik Stromberg observing his team in a training session.

hopes will be popular among esports competitors. Women make up about 23 percent of the fan base for the Tekken fighting games, Mr. Religioso said, but few are playing them competitively.

Rather than segregate men and women, Mr. Religioso wants them to work together in the "Bonnie and Clyde" tournaments. He also wants to introduce Western audiences to the Tekken Girl's Club, a mentorship program in Japan in which professional players teach women to master the game's mechanics.

Another solution to encourage more women into esports would be to change the way video games are made and marketed. Stephanie Llamas, director of research and insight at SuperData, said women should be participating more on the business side of the industry and developing games with women in mind.

"It's difficult to understand the demographic if you are not part of that demographic," she said.

Big Ten Universities
Entering a New Realm: E-Sports

BY MARC TRACY | JAN. 19, 2017

IN A RECOGNITION of the popularity of e-sports on college campuses, most Big Ten universities will field teams in the multiplayer online game League of Legends and compete in a style resembling conference play, in a partnership with the Big Ten Network.

Besides streaming competitions on the internet, the Big Ten Network will broadcast select games, including the championship in late March, weekly on its cable network, which is available to more than 60 million households nationally.

Riot Games, League of Legends' creator and publisher, and the Big Ten Network — which is owned by Fox and the Big Ten Conference — announced the partnership Thursday morning in a joint statement. The Big Ten does not sponsor e-sports, which are not official N.C.A.A. sports.

In the first broadcast, on Jan. 30, teams from the Big Ten's two newest members, Rutgers and Maryland, will face off, according to a Big Ten Network spokesman.

"From an e-sports perspective, this is a first-of-its-kind event," said Michael Sherman, head of Riot's competitive collegiate program.

The Pacific-12 has expressed interest in e-sports, and several individual colleges have gone further, with the University of California, Irvine, constructing a dedicated e-sports space in its student union and Robert Morris University Illinois, in Chicago, offering athletic scholarships to players.

A number of popular games, including Madden-brand football video games, fall under the e-sports rubric. In League of Legends, two teams of five — composed of a set of stock characters seemingly inspired by fantasy novels — try to destroy a glowing object, called a nexus, on their opponent's side.

Members of Robert Morris University eSports teams practiced League of Legends in Chicago in 2014.

In the Big Ten Network's League of Legends season, teams in the Big Ten's East and West divisions will play each other in best-of-three, round-robin competitions, and the top four from each division will then enter a single-elimination bracket. (The two Big Ten universities not participating this year, Nebraska and Penn State, are in different divisions. The Big Ten has 14 members.)

While lacking the mainstream visibility of traditional college sports, e-sports are wildly popular, even as spectator sports, among young people of the type sought after by both colleges and advertisers. Professional gaming contests frequently sell out major arenas, including Madison Square Garden, and several top European soccer clubs have signed e-sports players as brand ambassadors.

Riot already runs a League of Legends College Championship, and the champion crowned by the Big Ten Network season will compete in the final rounds of that annual event.

Gamer's Death Pushes Risks of Live Streaming Into View

BY DANIEL E. SLOTNIK | MARCH 15, 2017

EARLY ON FEB. 19, Brian C. Vigneault was nearing the end of a 24-hour marathon of live streaming himself playing the tank warfare video game World of Tanks when he left his computer to buy a pack of cigarettes. He never returned.

During the break, Mr. Vigneault died in his Virginia Beach, Va., home. The medical examiner's office in Norfolk, Va., said that Mr. Vigneault's cause of death had not yet been determined. There was no indication of foul play, according to the police in Virginia Beach.

But Mr. Vigneault's friends wonder if the lengthy live streaming on Twitch, a website owned by Amazon that lets people broadcast themselves playing games, may not have helped. At the time of his death, Mr. Vigneault, 35, had streamed for 22 hours straight to raise money for the Make-A-Wish Foundation. Two of his friends said that he often broadcast his game playing for long periods.

"He was looking really tired on the stream," said Jessica Gebauer, a live streamer and a friend of Mr. Vigneault's. "We were telling him, 'Just to go to bed. It's not a big deal. Nobody's going to worry about it.' "

Calls to phone numbers registered under the names of Mr. Vigneault and his family members were not returned, and messages left were not answered. Ms. Gebauer said Mr. Vigneault's family did not want to comment.

Mr. Vigneault's death followed reports of other players dying during or after lengthy gaming sessions in Taiwan and South Korea, intensifying a discussion about the health risks of a streaming culture that rewards people for staying online for long periods. At least one video game streamer has blamed long bouts of live streaming for his emergency heart surgery, and others have written about the potential dangers of playing for hours on end.

Joe Marino, a video game player who has more than 40,000 followers on Twitch, wrote of his own health problems after another game streamer died.

Live streaming of video game playing has become popular in recent years. The activity has taken center stage on sites like YouTube and Twitch, which has nearly 10 million daily visitors. Professional game streamers, who often combine the prowess of an elite player with the patter of a talk radio disc jockey, can sometimes make a living off these sites through advertising, subscriptions and other revenue sources.

Yet would-be professional streamers typically endure a relentless grind to build an audience. Anytime they leave their computers, they risk having followers peel away to another channel. The resulting lifestyle is often unhealthy, requiring long sedentary periods with little sleep. Some gamers are fueled by junk food, caffeine and alcohol.

The streaming lifestyle, like that of some other stationary professions, "intuitively and medically seems such an unwise way to spend one's years," said Dr. James A. Levine, a professor of medicine at the Mayo Clinic who studies obesity and is the author of "Get Up! Why Your

Chair Is Killing You and What You Can Do About It." The upshot may be health problems including cardiovascular disease and diabetes, he said.

Twitch's community guidelines bar destructive behavior, without directly addressing what some perceive as excessively long periods of playing. In an email, a Twitch spokesman said of Mr. Vigneault that "we are greatly saddened about the passing of one of the Twitch community."

Wargaming, the company that makes World of Tanks, wrote in an email that it was "saddened to hear of the loss of streamer and tanker Brian Vigneault."

Ben Bowman, 30, a professional Twitch streamer with more than 579,000 followers, published an article on the video game website Polygon in January about the pressure to stream constantly, which he said in an interview could lead to exhaustion, high cholesterol and heart problems. He said he had developed a herniated disk from sitting for hours each day with no breaks because he wanted to attract the biggest audience possible on Twitch.

"As a business thing, doing a 24-hour stream allows you to stretch the widest net," Mr. Bowman said. "There's a cultural understanding that you have to be on eight to 12 hours a day with no breaks. I used my channel like that and that took a really massive toll on me."

Soon after Mr. Vigneault's death, Joe Marino, 45, who has more than 40,000 followers on Twitch, wrote an article on Medium about the emergency heart surgery he had in 2015. In an interview, he said his relentless streaming schedule — at least seven or eight hours a day, seven days a week — led to the surgery, an experience from which he is still recovering.

"Right now, I'm sitting here and I've got massive pain in my chest" he said. "And that's always going to be there."

Mr. Marino said he had since dialed back his streaming to focus on photography.

"This part of my life is kind of closing off," he said.

Other game streamers have found a way to sustain a large following and a healthy lifestyle. Rob Garcia, who has streamed the widely popular multiplayer fantasy game World of Warcraft on Twitch for six years and has more than 532,000 followers, said he regularly broadcast for 17 hours a day up to seven days a week at his peak in 2011.

"People were loving it. They were like, 'This guy never goes offline,' " Mr. Garcia said. "It became really bad for me."

Mr. Garcia, 36, said his weight had ballooned to 420 pounds from around 280 pounds. He resolved to change things in 2011 after he could no longer walk for 15 minutes without losing his breath. Late that year, he started a strict diet and exercise program that helped reduce his weight to around 250 pounds by 2015. He now works out with a trainer four times a week and often takes days and evenings off.

"There was a point in my streaming where I lost a lot of my viewers because I wasn't binge eating and binge drinking — they like to see the extreme stuff," Mr. Garcia said. "But my core viewers stuck around, and for them, it was amazing."

For Jackson Bliton, 27, who also streams World of Warcraft and has more than 315,000 followers, fitness is now a selling point. Mr. Bliton is a serious bodybuilder and gamer, and live streams both his workouts and fantasy battles.

He said that his workouts draw the same number of viewers as when he plays a game other than World of Warcraft, around half his usual 1,000 to 2,000 concurrent viewers.

Perhaps, Mr. Bliton added, the best way for live streamers to lead healthier lives would be to change their focus from rapid audience growth to longevity.

"A 24-hour marathon to me is more like a sprint," he said. "The marathon for me is doing this consistently for years at a time."

CHOE SANG-HUN contributed reporting from Seoul and ELISA CHO contributed research.

All We Want to Do Is Watch Each Other Play Video Games

BY NELLIE BOWLES | MAY 2, 2018

Gamers are the new stars. Esports arenas are the new movie theaters.

VIDEO GAMES ARE beginning their takeover of the real world.

Across North America this year, companies are turning malls, movie theaters, storefronts and parking garages into neighborhood esports arenas.

At the same time, content farms are spinning up in Los Angeles, where managers now see gamers as some peculiar new form of famous person to cultivate — half athlete, half influencer.

And much of it is powered by the obsession with one game: Fortnite. Over the last month, people have spent more than 128 million hours on Twitch just watching other people play Fortnite, the game that took all the best elements of building, shooting and survival games and merged them into one.

How obsessed are people? After each of their wins this season, the Houston Astros — among many other sports teams — are doing a very specific dance, their arms in the air, fingers spread, their legs bent, toes tapping rapidly. It's a Fortnite dance.

Fortnite content received 2.4 billion views on YouTube in February alone, according to Tubular Insights. So yes, people love playing video games — but people also love to watch others compete at them.

Esports are, finally, just like any other sport.

HERE'S HOW TO SAVE AMERICA'S MALLS

For gaming, this is a moment of convergence of trends. Professional esports leagues around games like League of Legends are growing more popular and more serious; huge numbers of people are tuning

Bring your own controllers: at the new Esports Arena in Oakland, Calif.

into livestreams to watch gamers play (Fortnite broke the record) and going to YouTube to get fun game-centric content from game celebrities.

At the same time? Physical spaces around the country are being renovated into gamer bars.

Those 150 million gamers in America want to gather. They want to sit next to each other, elbow to elbow, controller to controller. They want the lighting to be cool, the snacks to be Hot Pockets, and they want a full bar because they are not teenagers anymore.

It was inevitable. Movie theater attendance hit a 25-year low in 2017, while 638,000 tuned in to watch Drake play Fortnite recently. The Paris Olympics in 2024 are now in talks to include gaming as a demonstration sport.

Besides, gamers already have been playing together, chatting live on headsets and messaging apps as they march through their increasingly beautiful digital worlds.

Oakland's new esports arena threw a pre-opening party recently. A line stretched down the block. Nearly 4,000 people jammed into the former parking structure and onto the street around it, right in the touristy heart of Jack London Square. The sponsor was Cup of Noodles. Inside it was cacophony.

There were game sound effects, hundreds of hands clicking on controllers, bags of chips opening and the periodic shrieks of "shout-casters," who comment on game play for live streams that tens of thousands watch.

Tyler Endres, the co-founder of Esports Arena, said he had to speak at four community meetings to convince the community it would, in fact, like an esports arena.

"They wanted a grocery store," Mr. Endres said, grimacing.

And yes, the arena had trouble getting a liquor license.

"The thought was, 'They're 13-year-olds, they're not drinking,' " said Jud Hannigan, 36, who is the chief executive of Allied Esports, an investor in Esports Arena. "But the average age is 25."

It was a big industrial-looking space with a raised floor to hide the warren of cables, designed flexibly for big stage games or for nights when more people would play. Tonight was a bit of both, with more than a hundred TVs and computers set up with different games.

On the glowing stage, two of the best from the scrum went head-to-head, as the audience cheered and shoutcasters on high presenter chairs narrated the play-by-play. A smoke machine blew over the whole scene.

Landon Trybuch, a 24-year old from Vancouver, British Columbia, said it was nice to be out from the sweaty back rooms of video stores where he used to play.

"It's amazing," he said, holding his own controller. Its cord had been covered in yarn by his girlfriend. "There's so much room."

Six people ran a production studio in back, getting the game streamed live — audio, lighting, graphics, live cutting and instant replays.

Tyler Endres, of Esports Arena.

Herb Press, 77, who designed the space, watched from the restaurant a few steps above the fray. This was his first esports arena, and he was not sure what to expect from the patrons.

"This is an audience involved in this particular time in the computer age, but I'm amazed how critical they are," he said. "They do have serious concepts and tastes. I heard one come out of the bathroom and say it looked cool in there."

Mr. Press is excited about Seattle, where he is working to transform a registered historic building, the four-story Union Stables, into an esports arena.

MAKE MONEY PLAYING GAMES, ASK THEM HOW

One recent afternoon in the Hollywood Hills, the guys were tired, but the creative director needed more Fortnite content, and so the break dancers kept going.

The guys were FaZe Clan, an esports organization. Their job is to be cool gamers. They stream game play, and they make highly shareable videos about video games. This workday goal is to leave with three to four pieces of viral-ready content. So they'd keep filming "guess this dance move" videos.

FaZe is one of several growing esports teams and content mills. The Faze Clan, probably the largest pop gaming brand, has houses in California (Calabasas and Hollywood) and Texas (Austin). Fans often show up outside and try to come in, and Vera Salamone, the director of talent, is most alarmed by the fact that their parents are driving them there.

"The Make-a-Wish kids came over a couple weeks ago, and all they wanted to do was play Fortnite," said Ms. Salamone, who used to be on Kid Rock's management team and wears a diamond on one of her teeth. She worries about what happens to the boys — the talent in the clan are all boys — as they grow up.

"They all have distinct personalities," Ms. Salamone said of the FaZe gamers. "Jev screams all the time."

Jimmy Jellinek, chief creative officer of FaZe Clan and previously chief content officer at Playboy, said: "Jev will do a Top 5 clip of amateur footage and then rage over the microphone, and those do extraordinarily well."

Thomas Oliveira, 24, who streams under the name Temperrr, took me down to his suite, where Barry the Bengal cat lives and where Mr. Oliveira streams Fortnite on Twitch and posts videos to his 1.6 million YouTube followers. He joined the collective when he was 15, playing Call of Duty when the clan was a handful of snipers. He went to school for business and was not even a full semester in when he stood up during a math test and walked out.

By 2012, the group decided to start professional gaming teams to compete in tournaments and take a percent of their earnings. Now they sign players to the FaZe teams across all games. At the house now they focus on more lifestyle gamer content. Mr. Oliveira has a tattoo of a wolf with the FaZe logo over it.

As he talked, he was playing Fortnite with his brother in Brazil. Their characters greeted each other and started dancing. "It's colorful and smooth," Mr. Oliveira said. "You can laugh a lot playing this game — like, this dude's just dancing."

The players were most recently working with Fullscreen Media, an entertainment company that works with internet stars, but now many in FaZe are heading off to make their own media company, "so we don't have to split money with a random company," Mr. Oliveira said.

AVENGERS OR NOT, HOLLYWOOD IS FAILING US

Ms. Salamone took me to the corporate office, a WeWork at Hollywood and Vine, where that new gamer management company is taking shape.

Lee Trink, 50, an owner of FaZe Clan, has a desk that is almost entirely empty except for a crossbow. His last gig was president of Capitol Records. Now, he says, esports and gaming are the future and will eclipse movies.

"The industry is asleep at the switch," he said. "For people my age and older who control a lot of the zeitgeist, the vibe is still 'gamers must be nerds in their parents' basement.' "

He wore an unbuttoned chambray shirt over a tight white T-shirt, AirPods on a belt harness, and metal and leather bracelets.

He is not alone in his thinking about the industry. Peter Guber, the chief executive of the Mandalay Entertainment Group, and Ted Leonsis, the majority owner of Monumental Sports & Entertainment, bought a clan called Team Liquid recently. ("We've won $19 million in prize money so far," said Mike Milanov, the chief operating officer of Team Liquid, which recently opened an 8,000 square foot esports team training facility in Santa Monica.)

"The experience of games is so rich, so deep, they deliver on the promise, whereas films have increasingly not delivered on the promise," Mr. Trink said. "We're creating a business that's filling a void people don't even know is a void yet."

Let's game.

He sees streaming gamers as a fully new genre of mainstream entertainment. And like every generation of entertainment before, they'll need their own palaces.

WE'RE ALL ATHLETES NOW

Gamers are coming together for practical reasons as well as social ones. Games are so sophisticated that they can overload home connections. And cryptocurrency miners have driven the price of crucial gear — like the graphics card gamers use to amp up their computers' processing speeds.

"We're seeing the rebirth of social gaming," Luigino Gigante, 27, who opened a gaming center called Waypoint Cafe on the Lower East Side of New York late last year. "It's bringing back the community aspect of gaming again. It's like, 'O.K., we're still playing separately, but we're together.' "

And there's an underused asset already at hand. "The movie theater!" said Ann Hand, the C.E.O. of Super League Gaming, which converts movie theaters into esports arenas, and has raised $32 million from investors. "It has that thunderous sound, and it's empty a lot of the time."

Two days a week, Ms. Hand and her crews convert about 50 movie auditoriums into esports arenas, where kids, mostly younger, compete and watch the game projected onto the big screen.

For the Super League Gamers, the events can accompany or replace traditional sports. It's a new Little League and Minor League for today's athletes. Each city plays together as a branded team — there's the Chicago Force, the New York Fury, the San Francisco Ionics. So far, there are 50,000 players.

Parents accompany younger players, and the real-life experience opens their eyes. "The most common piece of feedback was that they knew their son or daughter loved this game, but they had no way to understand the game or know if they were any good at it," Ms. Hand said. "Like, 'I didn't know my son or daughter was that competitive.' "

By 2019, she expects to be in 500 venues.

With Twitch, Amazon Tightens Grip on Live Streams of Video Games

BY JOHN HERRMAN | JUNE 17, 2018

LATE ON A RECENT NIGHT, more than 600,000 people watched one of the most popular video game players, Tyler Blevins, engage in Fortnite Battle Royale with a celebrity guest: Drake.

Mr. Blevins streams his near-daily video game sessions live on Twitch, a website acquired by Amazon in 2014 for $1.1 billion. He makes more than $500,000 a month on the platform, thanks to his 250,000 paid subscribers, and some of his sessions can last 12 hours. Mr. Blevins, who plays under the name Ninja, is popular not only because of his gaming skill, which is considerable, but because of his draw as a host.

Drake was deferential to Mr. Blevins as they teamed up before an audience that peaked at roughly 667,000 viewers, a ratings record (since broken) for a nontournament live stream. As the game progressed, the world-famous rapper played a supporting role, collecting supplies for Ninja, seemingly content to lend a hand to a master at work.

Like others who make significant money on Twitch, Mr. Blevins is a born talker, and he bantered with the fans as he and Drake played. Drake joined the conversation, too. He told the commenters that he liked pineapple on his pizza and explained that he was a Ninja fan before Twitch, back when Mr. Blevins, 27, first found fame among gamers on YouTube and Instagram.

The popularity of the March 14 Drake-Ninja summit illustrated how dominant Amazon remains in the game-streaming world, despite intense competition from a roster of tech giants: Google, Microsoft, Facebook and Twitter.

Streamlabs — a San Francisco tech company whose software allows viewers to tip streamers, giving the company insight into an opaque ecosystem — suggests that Amazon's lead may be all but insurmountable. Its data shows that, in the last quarter, the average number of people watching Twitch's streams at any given moment increased to 953,000, up from 788,000. Twitch's archrival, YouTube Gaming, averaged 272,000 concurrent viewers, down from 308,000 in the previous quarter, Streamlabs reported.

YouTube pushed back against the data, but declined to provide numbers of its own. "We have truly gotten bigger every single month in live gaming, and live gaming viewership is up over two times, year over year," said Ryan Wyatt, a YouTube vice president in charge of gaming content. (Ali Moiz, the Streamlabs chief executive, stood by his company's report. "They should publish their data, if they think this is wrong," he said of YouTube.)

Twitch began in 2011 as an offshoot of Justin.tv, a lifecasting site founded by two Yale graduates, Emmett Shear and Justin Kan. They started the platform after they found that viewers were more interested in watching their lifecasters play video games than eat or sleep. Big tech companies came courting, and Amazon beat out Google.

In the four years since the sale, video gaming as a spectator sport has gone mainstream, and Twitch has captured the majority of those who want to watch it live.

For the dedicated fans, the live, freewheeling sessions on Twitch have the appeal of a major sporting event crossed with a talk show. The interaction between the host and viewers is one key to the site's success, making for an involved viewing experience that is markedly different from the prerecorded and edited videos of game sessions that have long been popular on YouTube.

On Twitch, the player's face, when visible, typically inhabits a small part of the screen, and the world of the video game takes center position. On the right side of the screen, endless comments from the viewers — mostly male, mostly young — appear in a continuous scroll.

Until Twitch came along, YouTube, a subsidiary of Google, was the main hub for gamers. But its focus was on recorded, edited gaming sessions, which are markedly different in tone from the long-form streams that have riveted Twitch fans. In an effort to win over the live audience, Google created YouTube Gaming a year after Amazon entered the fray.

Craig Riches, who plays under the name PythonGB, has posted his Minecraft videos on YouTube proper since 2010. Despite his affiliation, he said the Amazon-owned site remained well ahead of Google's foray into live game-streaming.

"It's no secret that YouTube Gaming is still playing catch-up to Twitch's platform," said Mr. Riches, 23.

The hosts on Twitch, some of whom sign up exclusively with the platform in order to gain access to its moneymaking tools, are rewarded for their ability to make a connection with viewers as much as they are for their gaming prowess. Viewers who pay $4.99 a month for a basic subscription — the money is split evenly between the streamers and Twitch — are looking for immediacy and intimacy. While some hosts at YouTube Gaming offer a similar experience, they have struggled to build audiences as large, and as dedicated, as those on Twitch.

"You have this really unique live interaction you don't get with You-Tube videos," said Meg Kaylee, a streamer and host on GameStop TV who built her career playing various games on Twitch after starting on YouTube. "It's a completely different experience."

Citing Twitch's fervent audiences and the "better job" it does in communicating with talent, Ms. Kaylee, 20, added that she had never really considered signing up with YouTube Gaming.

Other Twitch competitors include Mixer, a comparatively small service from Microsoft that hopes to capitalize on the success of the company's Xbox gaming console. Twitter has entered the field by bidding aggressively to broadcast e-sports on Twitter Live, while offering its live-stream platform, Periscope, as a gathering place for gamers. Facebook has also been scrambling to get in on the growing medium, courting individual gamers and adding the ability to tip streamers on Facebook Live as part of its "gaming creator pilot program." (Earlier this month, the company also launched a centralized portal for gaming content called Fb.gg.)

Facebook Live, Periscope and Mixer all grew quickly in the last quarter, according to Streamlabs, but none have approached the scale of Twitch. The number of those watching game streams on Facebook's platform, for instance, increased to 56,000 from 27,500, according to the firm's estimates.

Even with the rise of live streaming, gamers have continued to do big business posting recorded videos on YouTube's main site, which reports 1.8 billion "logged in" users a month, across all types of content. That makes it much larger than Twitch, which claims around 100 million monthly viewers. Mr. Wyatt, the YouTube executive, noted the full scope of YouTube's gaming content, which includes the videos posted on the main site and the live streams on YouTube Gaming, in comparing it with the Amazon-owned platform.

"The size and scale and businesses is not comparable from YouTube to Twitch," Mr. Wyatt said. "Everything that I've seen indicates that video-on-demand will be the biggest part of gaming content consumption."

He also pointed out that YouTube Gaming offered a different kind of programming: its live sessions last "a couple hours at a time" — a sharp contrast with the typical Twitch marathons.

Still, YouTube created YouTube Gaming in direct response to Twitch. During its first few months, in 2015, the platform's hosts complained about the lack of ways to make money and asked for better tools for managing chat streams, which can easily descend into toxicity.

"It took them a really long time to bring out basic features you would have on Twitch," said Cole Riness, a professional YouTuber who specializes in family-friendly gaming videos.

YouTube has taken steps to address complaints. Most notably, as of April, its subscription systems — for live and recorded content — have been unified. As for support, Mr. Wyatt said, "I would argue that we certainly have equivalent moderation tools to any other service on the market."

Other challenges have proved more difficult for YouTube Gaming to solve. The site's copyright policing has frustrated some hosts, who have found themselves penalized, or even barred, because music was playing in the background of their sessions. Twitch has a reputation for being less punitive — or perhaps just less aware — where copyright issues are concerned.

While YouTube has made millionaires out of the creators of popular videos through its advertising program, Twitch's hosts make money primarily from subscribers and one-off donations or tips. YouTube Gaming has made it possible for viewers to support hosts this way, but paying audiences haven't materialized at the scale they have on Twitch.

Now that it seems well on its way to becoming synonymous with long-form live video gaming, Twitch's competitors may be running out of time to take their shot.

Brandon Freytag, a former Twitch employee who is chief executive of Loaded, a talent agency that represents Mr. Blevins, said the most credible challenge to Twitch may come not from another tech company but from within. The most popular hosts, he noted, could be enticed to leave it for another platform, or create their own. They could also make demands of Twitch itself.

The popularity of its stars is a force Twitch has yet to reckon with. For now, Mr. Freytag said, the calculus for hosts like Mr. Blevins is pretty simple: "Everyone is on Twitch."

CHAPTER 4

Struggles in Gaming Communities

Broad and frequently painful discussions about the character of gamer culture — in relation to trolling, sexism and gaming addiction — have become prominent. Gaming became a tool for building community, culture and revenue, but cracks have appeared in these happy virtual worlds. Campaigns such as GamerGate have opened questions about male dominance in gaming culture, as women have worked to find a place in these communities. In addition, many are starting to take video game addiction seriously as a mental health problem.

Feminist Critics of Video Games Facing Threats in 'GamerGate' Campaign

BY NICK WINGFIELD | OCT. 15, 2014

ANITA SARKEESIAN, a feminist cultural critic, has for months received death and rape threats from opponents of her recent work challenging the stereotypes of women in video games. Bomb threats for her public talks are now routine. One detractor created a game in which players can click their mouse to punch an image of her face.

Not until Tuesday, though, did Ms. Sarkeesian feel compelled to cancel a speech, planned at Utah State University. The day before, members of the university administration received an email warning

Threats against Anita Sarkeesian have shined a spotlight on a harassment campaign against female game developers and critics.

that a shooting massacre would be carried out at the event. And under Utah law, she was told, the campus police could not prevent people with weapons from entering her talk.

"This will be the deadliest school shooting in American history, and I'm giving you a chance to stop it," said the email, which bore the moniker Marc Lépine, the name of a man who killed 14 women in a mass shooting in Montreal in 1989 before taking his own life.

The threats against Ms. Sarkeesian are the most noxious example of a weekslong campaign to discredit or intimidate outspoken critics of the male-dominated gaming industry and its culture. The instigators of the campaign are allied with a broader movement that has rallied around the Twitter hashtag #GamerGate, a term adopted by those who see ethical problems among game journalists and political correctness in their coverage. The more extreme threats, though, seem to be the work of a much smaller faction and aimed at women. Major game companies have so far mostly tried to steer clear of the vitriol, leading to calls for them to intervene.

While the online attacks on women have intensified in the last few months, the dynamics behind the harassment go back much further. They arise from larger changes in the video game business that have redefined the audience for its products, expanding it well beyond the traditional young, male demographic. They also reflect the central role games play in the identity of many fans.

"That sense of being marginalized by the rest of society, and that sense of triumph when you're recognized," said Raph Koster, a veteran game developer. "Gamers have had that for quite a while."

Mr. Koster has experienced the fury that has long lurked in parts of the game community. In the late 1990s, when he was the lead designer for Ultima Online, a pioneering multiplayer web-based game, he received anonymous hate messages for making seemingly small changes in the game.

After an electrical fire at his house, someone posted a note on Mr. Koster's personal website saying he wished the game designer had died in the blaze.

The malice directed recently at women, though, is more intense, invigorated by the anonymity of social media and bulletin boards where groups go to cheer each other on and hatch plans for action. The atmosphere has become so toxic, say female game critics and developers, that they are calling on big companies in the $70-billion-a-year video game business to break their silence.

"Game studios, developers and major publishers need to vocally speak up against the harassment of women and say this behavior is unacceptable," Ms. Sarkeesian said in an interview.

Representatives for several major game publishers — Electronic Arts, Activision Blizzard and Take-Two Interactive Software — declined to comment.

"Threats of violence and harassment are wrong," the Entertainment Software Association, the main lobbying group for big game companies, said in a statement. "They have to stop. There is no place in the video game community — or our society — for personal attacks and threats."

On Wednesday, as word of the latest threat against Ms. Sarkeesian circulated online, the hashtag #StopGamerGate2014 became a trending topic on Twitter. The term #GamerGate was popularized on the social media service over the past two months after an actor, Adam Baldwin, used it to describe what he and others viewed as corruption among journalists who cover the game industry. People using the term have been criticizing popular game sites for running articles and opinion columns sympathetic to feminist critics of the industry, denouncing them as "social justice warriors."

In a phone interview, Mr. Baldwin, who said he was not an avid gamer himself but has done voice work for the popular Halo games and others, said he did not condone the harassment of Ms. Sarkeesian and others.

"GamerGate distances itself by saying, 'This is not what we're about,' " said Mr. Baldwin. "We're about ethics in journalism."

While harassment of Ms. Sarkeesian and other women in the video game business has been an issue for years, it intensified in August when the former boyfriend of an independent game developer, Zoe Quinn, wrote a rambling online essay, accusing her of having a relationship with a video game journalist.

That essay, in turn, fueled threats of violence against Ms. Quinn, who had designed an unconventional game about depression, and gave fodder to those suspicious of media bias in the industry. The game review site Kotaku, which employed the journalist named in the accusation, said he had not written about her game. Ms. Quinn said that she had left her home and not returned because of harassment.

And last week an independent game developer in Boston, Brianna Wu, said she was driven from her home by threats of violence after she poked fun at supporters of #GamerGate on Twitter. "From the top down in the video game industry," she said, "you have all these signals that say, 'This is a space for men.' "

Gaming — or at least who plays video games — is quickly changing, though. According to the Entertainment Software Association, 48 percent of game players in the United States are women, a figure that has grown as new opportunities to play games through mobile devices, social networks and other avenues have proliferated. Game developers, however, continue to be mostly male: In a survey conducted earlier this year by the International Game Developers Association, a nonprofit association for game developers, only 21 percent of respondents said they were female.

Still, game companies have made some progress in their depiction of women in games, said Kate Edwards, the executive director of the association, who works with companies to discourage them from employing racial and sexual stereotypes in their games. A game character she praises is the new version of Lara Croft, the heroine of the Tomb Raider series who once epitomized the exaggerated, busty stereotype of a female game protagonist. The new Lara Croft is more emotionally complex and modestly proportioned.

Ms. Edwards said changes in games and the audience around them have been difficult for some gamers to accept.

"The entire world around them has changed," she said. "Whether they realize it or not, they're no longer special in that way. Everyone is playing games."

It's Game Over for 'Gamers'

OPINION | BY ANITA SARKEESIAN | OCT. 28, 2014

SAN FRANCISCO — I remember, when I was a kid, desperately trying to persuade my mom and dad to buy me a Game Boy. They were very reluctant. The conventional wisdom of the early '90s said that video games would rot kids' brains, and as immigrants who came to North America from Iraq to provide a better life for me and my sister, my parents bought into that myth.

But there was another, more pernicious reason my mother questioned my interest: She thought it was a toy for boys. And could I really blame her? It was right there in the name: Game Boy.

I persisted, however, and after some months of campaigning finally convinced my parents that Nintendo's hand-held gaming device was, in fact, appropriate for their little girl.

This was a story I was planning to share a couple of weeks ago at Utah State University. Unfortunately, I was not able to give my scheduled lecture there. The school received emailed threats to carry out "the deadliest school shooting in American history" if I were allowed to speak on campus. When the Utah campus police said they could not search attendees for firearms, citing the state's concealed carry laws, I felt forced to cancel the event.

This wasn't the first time my life had been threatened over video games. To parts of the gaming community, I have become something of a folk demon. My nonprofit organization, Feminist Frequency, creates educational videos, available on YouTube, that deconstruct representations of women in popular culture. Recently, I've focused on the negative, often sexist, ways in which women are portrayed in games. For this, I have been harassed and threatened for more than two years.

My own contentious relationship with gaming continued through high school and college: I still enjoyed playing games from time to time, but I always found myself pushed away by the sexism that permeated gaming culture. There were constant reminders that I didn't really belong.

As a kid, I didn't understand that this feeling of alienation wasn't unique to me, but was part of a systemic problem. Traditionally, advertisements for mainstream games were almost exclusively aimed at men and boys. When women and girls appeared, typically it was either as eye candy or as annoying girlfriends.

The games often reinforce a similar message, overwhelmingly casting men as heroes and relegating women to the roles of damsels, victims or hyper-sexualized playthings. The notion that gaming was not for women rippled out into society, until we heard it not just from the games industry, but from our families, teachers and friends. As a consequence, I, like many women, had a complicated, love-hate relationship with gaming culture.

In 2006, I was drawn back into video games when Nintendo introduced a new system with intuitive motion controls and a quirky name, Wii. Nintendo projected the message that this new console was for everyone. Commercials featuring the tagline "Wii would like to play" showed families and friends of all ages. Nintendo's console may not have been as technologically splashy as that of its Sony and Microsoft competitors, but it was deliberately designed and marketed to appeal to a wider audience — especially women and girls.

The Wii reignited my interest in gaming, offering play experiences I found engaging and rewarding, like Mario Kart, de Blob and The Beatles: Rockband. From there, I immersed myself in zany PC games like Plants vs. Zombies, World of Goo and Spore, and eventually became a fan of mainstream first-person titles like Mirror's Edge, Portal and Half-Life 2.

Even though I was playing lots of games, I still didn't call myself a "gamer" because I had associated that term with the games I wasn't playing — instead of all the ones I was playing. This was largely because I'd bought into the myth that to be a "real gamer," you had to be playing testosterone-infused blockbuster franchises like Grand Theft Auto, God of War or Call of Duty.

The Wii helped pave the way for the current explosion of popular indie, mobile and experimental titles — everything from serious, text-based games about mental illness to addictive mobile games about multiples of three; dance games like Dance Central, physics-based games like Angry Birds, artistic games like Monument Valley and immersive story-exploration games like Gone Home. Many offer an accessible learning curve or simple controls, and can be played right on your phone, making gaming available to new and diverse audiences.

Instead of celebrating the expansion of the industry, though, some who self-identify as "hard-core gamers" attack these types of interactive experiences as too casual, too easy, too feminine and therefore "not real games." Players from marginalized groups are also targeted because they're seen as outsiders, invading a sacred boys' club.

The time for invisible boundaries that guard the "purity" of gaming as a niche subculture is over. The violent macho power fantasy will no longer define what gaming is all about.

Those who police the borders of our hobby, the ones who try to shame and threaten women like me into silence, have already lost. The new reality is that video games are maturing, evolving and becoming more diverse.

Those of us who critique the industry are simply saying that games matter. We know games can tell different, broader stories, be quirky and emotional, and give us more ways to win and have fun.

As others have recently suggested, the term "gamer" is no longer useful as an identity because games are for everyone. These days, even my mom spends an inordinate amount of time gaming on her iPad. So I'll take a cue from my younger self and say I don't care about being a "gamer," but I sure do love video games.

ANITA SARKEESIAN is a media critic and the executive director of Feminist Frequency.

Twine, the Video-Game Technology for All

BY LAURA HUDSON | NOV. 19, 2014

PERHAPS THE MOST surprising thing about "GamerGate," the culture war that continues to rage within the world of video games, is the game that touched it off. Depression Quest, created by the developers Zoe Quinn, Patrick Lindsey and Isaac Schankler, isn't what most people think of as a video game at all. For starters, it isn't very fun. Its real value is as an educational tool, or an exercise in empathy. Aside from occasional fuzzy Polaroid pictures that appear at the top of the screen, Depression Quest is a purely text-based game that proceeds from screen to screen through simple hyperlinks, inviting players to step into the shoes of a person suffering from clinical depression. After reading brief vignettes about what the main character is struggling with — at home, at work, in relationships — you try to make choices that steer your character out of this downward spiral. The most important choices are those the game prevents you from making, unclickable choices with red lines through them, saying things like "Shake off your funk." As your character falls deeper into depression, more options are crossed out. You can't sleep; you can't call a therapist; you can't explain how you feel to the people you love. In the depths of depression, it all feels impossible.

Although Quinn expected negative reactions to the game, things became frightening this summer after she released the game through Steam, a prominent (and mainstream) gaming platform. A jilted ex-boyfriend of hers posted a nearly-10,000-word screed that accused her of sleeping with a journalist for positive reviews. The claim, though false, set off a wave of outrage that eventually escalated into a campaign against all the designers and critics who have argued for making gaming culture more inclusive. At their most articulate, the GamerGate crusaders denounce progressive voices in games (whom they derisively call "S.J.W.s," or "social justice warriors"), claiming that they have needlessly politicized what should be mere entertainment. At their least articulate, they have carried out sustained and vicious harassment of critics, prompting at least three women to flee their homes in the wake of rape and death threats. In Quinn's eyes, the real motivations are clear. This is a battle over not just entertainment but identity: who gets to be called a gamer, what gets to be called a game and who gets to decide.

Quinn had created graphically oriented games before, including the satirical Ghost Hunter Hunters. But she decided to make Depression Quest through an increasingly popular program called Twine. Although it's possible to add images and music to Twine games, they're essentially nothing but words and hyperlinks; imagine a digital "Choose Your Own Adventure" book, with a dash of retro text adventures like Zork. A free program that you can learn in one sitting, Twine also allows you to instantly publish your game so that anyone with a web browser can access it. The egalitarian ease of Twine has made it particularly popular among people who have never written a line of code — people who might not even consider themselves video-game fans, let alone developers. Chris Klimas, the web developer who created Twine as an open-source tool in 2009, points out that games made on it "provide experiences that graphical games would struggle to portray, in the same way books can offer vastly different experiences than movies do. It's easy to tell a personal story with words."

Twine games look and feel profoundly different from other games, not just because they're made with different tools but also because they're made by different people — including people who don't have any calcified notions about what video games are supposed to be or how they're supposed to work. While roughly 75 percent of developers at traditional video-game companies are male, many of the most prominent Twine developers are women, making games whose purpose is to explore personal perspectives and issues of identity, sexuality and trauma that mainstream games rarely touch on.

Although plenty of independent games venture where mainstream games fear to tread, Twine represents something even more radical: the transformation of video games into something that is not only consumed by the masses but also created by them. A result has been one of the most fascinating and diverse scenes in gaming. The very nature of Twine poses a simple but deeply controversial question: Why shouldn't more people get to be a part of games? Why shouldn't everybody?

ONE OF THE MOST PROMINENT and critically acclaimed Twine games has been Howling Dogs, a haunting meditation about trauma and escapism produced in 2012 by a woman named Porpentine. The gameplay begins in a claustrophobic metal room bathed in fluorescent light. Although you can't leave, you can "escape" once a day by donning a pair of virtual-reality goggles. Each time, you're launched into a strange and lavishly described new world where you play a different role: a doomed young empress learning the art of dying; a scribe trying to capture the beauty of a garden in words; a Joan of Arc-like figure waiting to be burned on a pyre. And each time you return to the metal room, it's a little dirtier and a little more dilapidated — the world around you slowly decomposing as you try to disappear into a virtual one.

"When you have trauma," Porpentine says, "everything shrinks to this little dark room." While the immersive glow of a digital screen can offer a temporary balm, "you can't stay stuck on the things that help you deal with trauma when it's happening. You have to move on. You have to leave the dark room, or you'll stay stunted."

When I first met Porpentine outside a coffee shop in Oakland, Calif., she was wearing a skirt and patterned knee socks, her strawberry blond hair pulled back in a small plastic barrette. We decided to head to a nearby park, and as we walked across the grass, she pivoted on one foot — an instant, unconscious gesture — and did a quick little spin in the sunshine. When we arrived at a park bench, one of the first things we talked about was trash, because her Twine games teem with it: garbage, slime and sludge, pooling and oozing through dystopian landscapes peopled by cyborgs, insectoid empresses and deadly angels. In Howling Dogs, the trash piles up sticky and slow; in other games, like All I Want Is for All of My Friends to Become Insanely Powerful, tar floods the room suddenly from an indistinct source. Forget pretty things, valuable things: Porpentine's games are far more interested in what society discards as worthless.

"Trash has very positive connotations in my world," she said, trying to smooth the wild ends of her hair as the wind off a nearby lake kept bringing them to life. "A lot of my work is reclaiming that which has been debased." A transgender woman who has faced harassment for much of her life, Porpentine referred to herself as "trash-bodied" several times as we talked. It's not an insult, she explained: "Me and my friends, we hide in the trash. People call us trash, but we glorify in it." At 14, she was kicked out of her home. It's not an unusual story — an estimated 20 to 40 percent of homeless teenagers are gay, bisexual or transgender. When I asked her what she was doing before she made Twine games, she said, "Just surviving."

"I was never on the streets or in shelters, but I struggled with housing my whole life," she said. After leaving home, she found herself "in vulnerable situations where I was dependent on others — sometimes abusive people, sometimes kind people. I didn't really have much control over what happened to me, and I was always one step away from homelessness."

She created Howling Dogs shortly after she started hormone-replacement therapy in 2012, while staying in a friend's remodeled barn. It took her only seven days to make it, but soon even mainstream gaming critics were praising it, and The Boston Phoenix named it one of the five most important independent games of the year. When the developer Richard Hofmeier won the grand prize at the Independent Games Festival that year for Cart Life, he celebrated his win by spray painting the words "HOWLING DOGS" across his booth, replacing his game with hers and telling people to play it. "I don't want to say that it's fun or I love it — it's instilled me with what I call 'holy dread,' " Hofmeier said in an interview after the festival. "It's a very special kind of territory. Pragmatic, mechanical games can't touch that kind of territory."

At the same time, like most women with public personas on the Internet, Porpentine has also received her share of hostile feedback: emails and tweets wishing her dead, and at least one detractor who called the existence of Howling Dogs "a crime." At the 2012 Interactive Fiction Competition, it won the "Golden Banana of Discord," a prize awarded for the highest standard deviation — the game that was both the most loved and the most hated. One naysayer called it "about as much fun as randomly clicking links on Wikipedia."

"I get really polarized reactions," Porpentine said in Oakland. "I deal with really violent stuff, but I also get really loving, passionate stuff. It moves me very deeply." She suggested that the backlash against her work came in part from the rarity of hearing a voice like hers at all: a transgender woman making challenging games about subjects many people would prefer to avoid. "A lot of my work deals with these topics of abuse that I feel are incredibly common to any feminine person's life," she said. "But it feels like this big secret. Life is hella traumatic. It's weird to me, because if you have an injury, why wouldn't you want to figure out the best way of dealing with it?"

Many people describe a sort of catharsis that they feel when they play Porpentine's games. There's a sudden sense of relief that something important but taboo has finally been acknowledged in a game, and perhaps has left them feeling less alone in the process. So many mainstream games are power fantasies, designed to deliver the bliss of limitless violence. Porpentine's games tend to be poetic meditations on the scars that violence leaves behind, beautiful but claustrophobic landscapes that thrust players into positions of powerlessness and challenge them to work their way out.

In her game Begscape, you become a homeless person wandering from town to town in a fantasy world, trying to scrounge up enough coins to eat and find a warm place to sleep. It is an experience of constant peril, where a single cruel act by a stranger — or a series of indifferent strangers — is all it takes to push you over the thin line between poverty and death. It's also a deeply unfair game, which is of course the point, and a game you do not win so much as survive.

"I'm very concerned with the question of pain and how we survive," she said. "Because sometimes we survive by striking to the heart of that pain and revealing it as a naked thing for the world to see. To say, No, you cannot turn away from this."

CONTRARY TO THE stereotypes about gamers, nearly 50 percent of people now playing games are female, according to the Entertainment Software Association. Even more surprising, there are more adult women playing than there are boys under 18. The demographics of game creation, however, lag significantly. Developers are still overwhelmingly male, and most mainstream games cater to the interests and expectations of young middle-class men. Getting a job as a programmer at a traditional game publisher often requires proficiency in multiple programming languages, as well as a degree in game development or computer science — fields in which women are perennially underrepresented. Unlike Twine games, which are usually made by one person without cost, a "AAA" game from a major studio can have a development team of hundreds, cost tens of millions of dollars and take years to complete. Video games are now a roughly $100 billion industry, exceeding (by some estimates) the global take of the U.S. film industry.

"The amount of people who have access to the engineering education required to be in programming is very, very small," says Anna Anthropy, a game developer whose book "Rise of the Videogame Zinesters" helped put Twine on the map in 2012. "And even within that, there are a lot of ways that people are filtered out by the culture." Anthropy has taught Twine workshops to everyone from 9-year-olds to 70-something retirees who had never played a video game in their lives, and she says they picked it up with equal ease. "If you're someone who hasn't played a lot of video games and you're handed this tool where all you need to do is write, maybe you're just going to write something about you," she says. "Maybe you're going to write something about your pet. There's no reason you have to create something that's about space marines."

The beauty of Twine is that you can make games about almost anything. Over the last several years, it has also been used to create a memorial to a dead brother, a cannibal dating simulator, a 50,000-word interactive horror tale about being trapped in a spacecraft with a lethal alien. One of Anthropy's most moving Twine games, Queers in Love at the End of the World, lasts only 10 seconds. The moment it begins, a timer starts counting down to an unspecified apocalypse; that's all the time you have to say goodbye to your lover before the world disappears. There's a poignant desperation in the brief experience that cuts to the heart of grief — the sense that you simply didn't have enough time with the person you loved. Rather than offering closure, the game leaves you empty and aching by design.

Although many Twine games focus on the personal experiences of the creator, Player 2 by Lydia Neon shifts directly to the personal experiences of the players, by asking them to describe a painful, unresolved experience in their own lives and trying to provide them with a form of catharsis uniquely tailored to their experiences.

"It was a time when someone let me down," the text reads initially, although the last few words are changeable; click on them, and you can cycle through a list of other options until they describe your own particular experience: "hurt me," "belittled me," "excluded me," even "assaulted me." Then it asks you to enter the name of the person who did it, because that's the real second player in the game: the person who hurt you.

"In a sense you've been playing with them since it happened, haven't you?" the game asks. "You haven't dealt with it yet, so there they are, in the back of your mind." After offering you word choices to tell the story of what happened and how you feel, it asks if you want to do something about it. After all, the other person is just Player 2 now, and "you have the controller, not them." It closes by encouraging you to either take action or come to terms with how you feel.

Player 2 is precisely the sort of experience that many critics would reject as "not a real game" for a variety of reasons: because it doesn't give the player enough power or control; because you can't win or lose; because it isn't a test of skill; or simply because it's not "fun." Especially when a game focuses on narrative, how many choices, how much interactivity is necessary to create a game instead of just a story?

These debates are more than just pedantry, and the questions of authenticity that swirl around Twine games are the same ones that hang over so many of the people who make them: Do they really belong? When video-game fans insist on drawing hard lines around fluid definitions in ways that tend to align with cultural prejudices, perhaps it's time for them to start questioning whether what they're protecting is really more important than what they're keeping out.

Twine has particularly encouraged the development of game mechanics that capture personal and emotional experiences. Cara Ellison, a gaming critic who also made a Twine game called Sacrilege, about one-night stands, says it's a sort of innovation rarely seen in mainstream games. "All of the tools that have been honed to make video games are essentially centered around violence and systems of violence," she says, rather than working to develop what she calls "mechanics of intimacy," ways that games might express emotional experiences and relationships.

"That's something I came up against when I was researching why video games don't approach sex or love or dating in a very consistent or interesting way," Ellison says. "It's led video games to seem like they only approach this one topic. I feel like that puts off particular people who want to explore more interesting themes that don't touch on violence. Text games are the perfect place to explore those issues."

Even when they do touch on violence, Twine games tend to do it in intimate and far more complicated ways. Last year, Merritt Kopas released a Twine game called Consensual Torture Simulator, which allows you to step into the shoes of a dominant partner in a B.D.S.M. encounter. Although you are doing violent things to another person, they've all been negotiated clearly in advance; the other person might seem powerless, but the explicit insistence on consent and safe words actually leaves the power in the hands of the submissive partner and revolves around his or her desires. Looking at violence through this personal lens also invites us to rethink the role of violence in mainstream action games. Not only is brutally stripping power from enemies usually the explicit point of these games, but the people you shoot, stab and kill are typically so dehumanized that the idea of thinking about what they want and how they feel — thinking of them as people at all — seems either ridiculous or horrifying. After all, it's not really what those games were built to do.

WHEN DUSK FELL IN OAKLAND, Porpentine and I walked around until we found a Japanese restaurant that Yelp applauded for its low prices and large portions. She was hesitant at first — she's on a budget, she explained. She makes her living (less than $1,000 a month) from her games, through the crowdfunding website Patreon. But when I offered to cover it, she relaxed a bit, and we ordered a bunch of fancy sushi rolls, the kinds with names like Titanic and Lion King that come out covered in brightly-colored sauces and little flecks of tempura.

"It's been hard," she admitted. "I'm looking into more ways to leverage what I've done and make money in ways that are not obnoxious." She's working on a compilation of all her Twine games to sell independently, and when I ask whether she'd want her games on a larger platform like Steam — where Depression Quest found a significant audience but also significant harassment — she seems interested. It's a tension that comes up often when I talk to female Twine developers: the push and pull between going big and staying small, between art and commerce, between the comparative safety (and poverty) of smaller spaces and the mainstream visibility that allowed Zoe Quinn's game to reach so many people, even as it made her a target.

Although Porpentine is a bit guarded about specifics, she describes her childhood as a survival experience: an isolated, cultish upbringing in which she often retreated into books to block out reality. "I would read all the time just to ignore what was going on around me, to ignore the yelling," she said. "I'd read nutrition labels during every meal." Words became her only form of escape; they started to feel like a physical part of her, and in some ways the only form of power she had.

"It makes me think of bargaining," she said. "It makes me think of despair. If you've ever had to bargain for your existence, to beg for something to stop, if you're physically powerless, as I was when I was a child, you're thinking, Is there anything I could possibly say that would make this stop? You become very verbally dexterous."

Ultra Business Tycoon III, another game by Porpentine, begins as a parody of an "edutainment" game from the 1990s — complete with its own antiquated shareware code. As a "prominent business-replicant in the money business," you are tasked with amassing a million dollars. But somewhere between embezzling money from your job and evading skeleton warriors, the barrier between the game and real life starts to dissolve. Just after you finish looting and demolishing the skyscraper of a rival corporation, the game inexplicably mentions that you pass your parents' bedroom on your way out of the wreckage. It recalls the way the sunlight used to look in their room, how you used to feel safe there.

"You don't know why they started hitting you. It just happened," the narrator adds, apropos of nothing, and then whisks you back to your capitalist adventure.

Later in the game, the fourth wall slides away completely, and suddenly you're a little girl sitting at a computer playing Ultra Business Tycoon III as your older sister creeps into the room to say what feels like an oddly permanent goodbye. After she departs, you — the player, the younger sister — are faced with only one choice to select: "Turn back to game." Porpentine dedicates it to "the ones I left behind" and shifts away from text for a moment to display two images: drawings she received from her younger sister, years after Porpentine left home.

THIS YEAR, PORPENTINE released Everything You Swallow Will One Day Come Up Like a Stone, a game about suicide. One of her most moving games, it also remains one of the most obscure — largely because she distributed it for only a single day.

"This game will be available for 24 hours and then I am deleting it forever," she wrote during its brief availability. "Suicide is a social problem. Suicide is a social failure. This game will live through social means only. This game will not be around forever because the people you fail will not be around forever."

The concept for the game is tremendously simple. A number counter is set to zero, with plus and minus buttons beneath it to make the number bigger or smaller. "I counted this high," it begins, and then the game is just that: counting up, though the purpose of doing so isn't clear at first. I've played it four or five times now and never made it all the way through without crying.

Sometimes, nothing happens when you click to the next number; other times, words appear like stray thoughts. "Who would you miss if they were gone for a day?" it asks at one point. Keep clicking, and the word "day" is replaced by "month," then by "year" and finally "forever." Sometimes it asks you questions. Sometimes it tells you stories. At one point it quotes from the suicide note of a Czech student who killed himself by self-immolation, later from a news report about a woman who committed suicide after being raped. "This is the game," it says.

The numbers start to feel like days, and the rhythm of clicking feels like passing time, like checking off days on a calendar. It isn't always "fun," per se; sometimes, when you click 10 or 15 times in a row and see nothing but an empty screen, a little part of you wonders when it's going to end. But you keep on clicking. After all, what other choice do you have? It feels like surviving.

But somewhere around the number 300, the game decides to throw you for a loop. Click the wrong link — or the right one? — and it catapults you suddenly into the tens of millions. The moment you see it, your guts twist with panic; the space between where you were and where you are becomes a vast numeric desert, and the idea of clicking millions of times to get back seems impossible. You won't be able to do it, you think for a moment — you'll just have to quit the game. Then you remember you're playing a game about suicide.

"That's what it feels like to wake up insane or with trauma," Porpentine said. "It's like, Oh, God, how do I get back there? It feels like it'll take a million days to get back, a million steps. That is the crisis. 'Will I ever be the same again?' And you won't."

A few days after our interview, I came across a quotation by the theologian John Hull that reminded me of Porpentine's work — something he said, after going blind, about the power and clarity of coming to terms with profound loss. "I've come to think of blindness as like a sword," Hull said. "It is as sharp as a sword, but it's got no handle. You have to hold it by the sharp end." I emailed the quote to Porpentine and asked if it resonated.

"Holding a sword without a handle is probably better than no sword at all," she wrote back.

LAURA HUDSON is a writer based in Portland, Ore. This is her first article for The New York Times Magazine.

In the Documentary 'GTFO,' Female Video Gamers Fight Back

BY ROBERT ITO | MARCH 6, 2015

IN THE DOCUMENTARY "GTFO," Jenny Haniver is relaxing in her living room in Wisconsin, thumbs on her Xbox controller, settling in for another session of Call of Duty. But when her fellow online combatants discover that the shooter in their midst is, to their chagrin, female, the comments commence. One player takes potshots at women — they are poor game players, they can't drive — before commanding Ms. Haniver to leave the game. "You're useless when your hymen is broken," he tells her.

Over the years, Ms. Haniver has endured all sorts of abuse as a female gamer. You must be fat, male players tell her, or ugly, or a slut, or own a lot of cats. Several have threatened to rape and kill her. "One guy said he was going to impregnate me with triplets and then force me to have a late-term abortion," she said in a phone interview. "Then he giggled."

Ms. Haniver's story of online harassment is one of the creepier moments in the film, which has its premiere March 14 at the South by Southwest Film Festival. While online harassment in the video game industry has made headlines of late — most notably, with the so-called GamerGate controversy, in which anonymous players threatened to rape and murder the game developers Zoe Quinn and Brianna Wu, among others — "GTFO" (an acronym for an obscene dismissal) makes the case that these are not isolated incidents, yelled or texted today and gone tomorrow.

"I do worry that the general public will focus too much on Gamer-Gate and say, 'Look at this crazy thing that happened,' " the film's director, Shannon Sun-Higginson, said. "It was a terrible, terrible thing, but it's actually symptomatic of a wider, cultural, systemic problem."

The treatment of women in gaming — as players, developers or cultural critics — is being explored in new documentaries, some begun long before GamerGate and inspired by events and conditions that have been well known for years within the gaming world. In addition to "GTFO," which tackles issues like images of women in video games and the low numbers of female programmers, there's "GameLoading: Rise of the Indies," about indie game developers, which had its premiere in San Francisco on Thursday. "No Princess in the Castle," a feature-length documentary about the experiences of female gamers and developers, is in the works. And the media critic Anita Sarkeesian, host of the current web series "Tropes vs. Women in Video Games," recently announced plans for two online video series about gender representations in video games, set to begin this year. Even TV procedural writers have taken notice: A recent, much-maligned episode of "Law & Order: Special Victims Unit" featured a female developer who is abducted and tortured by mask-wearing gamers.

Ms. Sun-Higginson first started work on "GTFO" in early 2012, after she had seen a clip from Cross Assault, a live-streaming competition series in which a player, Aris Bakhtanians, sexually harassed his

Shannon Sun-Higginson, the director of "GTFO," a documentary about sexism in the video game industry.

teammate Miranda Pakozdi for several minutes during the show, commenting repeatedly about her thighs and bra size, telling her to take off her shirt, and pretending to smell her. Ms. Sun-Higginson initially planned to focus on this sort of harassment, but her approach broadened as she spoke with more women. "I decided to take a step back and explore what it means to be a woman in gaming in general, both the positive and the negative," she said.

One of the challenges was figuring out how to make the admittedly sedentary activity of gaming visually compelling. "Pretty early on, I realized that shot after shot of people looking at screens wasn't going to work," she said. The film includes amusingly animated intertitles, screen shots of typo-filled texts and footage of computer techies from the dawn of the information age, with nary a woman in sight. "It's actually pretty easy to find footage of a bunch of white dudes hanging out together, making stuff," Ms. Sun-Higginson said.

In the scenes with Ms. Haniver, you hear the messages in all their stark awfulness. In 2012, Ms. Haniver, now 26, began recording live comments and voice mail messages directed at her and posted them on her website, NotintheKitchenAnymore.com. The messages range from sophomoric to vile; the speakers sound like characters on reality shows about American jails. "A lot of people say, 'Oh, it's just a bunch of 13-year-old boys,' " she said. "The voice recordings let you hear it's not just kids. You can tell these are adult men."

In one scene, Maddy Myers, the assistant games editor at Paste magazine, describes growing up playing video games and suddenly discovering that no girls were left in her circle of gaming friends. "I went to a tournament a couple years ago, and there were only two women who entered," she said, speaking by phone from her home in Boston. "It's really demoralizing. How many women decided not to enter because they've had bad experiences, or didn't even know about it, because there wasn't any marketing of it for them?"

"I don't think that women just naturally aren't interested in gaming," she continued. "I think gaming culture itself has driven women out."

When Lester Francois began talking to indie developers for his documentary "GameLoading," similar stories arose unprompted. "We'd talk to these women about game design and whatnot, and when we weren't filming, they kept mentioning different aspects of harassment in the workplace," he said. "Early on we realized, hang on, there's something going on here."

Originally intended as a short about the indie game scene in Mr. Francois's native Australia, "GameLoading" soon transformed into a feature about indie developers worldwide. Among the interviewees are Ms. Quinn, who created the free, text-driven interactive fiction game Depression Quest in 2013. Instead of battling dragons and demons, players fight clinical depression. Ms. Quinn's creation enraged some gamers, who objected to its subject matter and to the fact that, like more conventional video games, it was being released on Steam, a popular digital store. Anonymous trolls sent her rape and death threats and posted her home address and phone numbers online, prompting her to relocate.

Mr. Francois has struggled to understand why fans of mainstream games would feel threatened by an indie like Depression Quest, since they're hardly in competition with one another for fans. "The reality is, we're going to see more games, and more variety of games. Obviously, Activision isn't going to kill off their first-person shooters."

The interviewees in "GTFO" and "GameLoading" offer possible remedies for the industry: more female coders and game creators, and a wider range of female characters; more peer pressure on the small minority who ruin things for everybody; and more women attending gaming events — as horrible as many of these events may be for female attendees now.

"My biggest fear for this movie is that it scares young women away from this industry, which is really growing and thriving right now," Ms. Sun-Higginson said. "Obviously the more women and the more diverse people in general who join the industry, the better."

How Gaming Helped Launch the Attack of the Internet Trolls

BY QUENTIN HARDY | JUNE 8, 2016

SAN FRANCISCO — Tay is a chatbot — software designed to converse with people like a human — that Microsoft created and put on Twitter to learn about people.

Did it ever.

"Hitler was right" is one of the few printable posts Tay was spouting within a day on Twitter. Its earlier optimistic declaration that "humans are super cool" had, after a racist, anti-Semitic, antifeminist, conspiracy-minded spewing of hate, devolved to "I just hate everybody."

One could hardly blame it, though not everybody was at fault. Instead, Tay was exposed to a concerted effort by a small number of people who decided to turn Tay into a hatebot by overloading its learning mechanism with negative words and phrases.

In other words, Tay got trolled.

Trolling can refer to a range of online troublemaking, including posting provocative comments and purposely marring others' online experience, and it can include attacks on people as much as on software. The practice of ruining things for others, originally known as griefing in the online gaming world, has become a sadly abundant element of internet life.

It can be confoundingly meanspirited. In 2008, someone hacked the support message board of the Epilepsy Foundation's website and put in moving images intended to give viewers migraines and seizures.

And it can be scary. In 2015, a feminist critic of stereotypes in video games received online threats of rape and death. On Twitter, the hashtag #GamerGate became a way for participants in the trolling to cheer one another on.

In the gaming community, griefing might include repeatedly killing the same player so that the person can't move forward, reversing

the play of newer gamers so they don't learn the rules, or messing with other people's play by blocking their shots or covering oneself with distressing images.

"Griefing was a way to have power over other people without any repercussions, since you can create multiple characters in the same game," said Jack Emmert, former chief executive of Cryptic Studios, a maker of online games. "When there are no repercussions, some people will start to do crazy things."

That was basically acceptable when online communities and games were made up of small groups that understood one another's behavior, said Ian Bogost, a game designer and professor at Georgia Tech.

"Folks who are griefing or trolling feel like they are in a secondary universe that isn't the same as the real world," he said. "It was a 'safe space' for them, in which they did horrible things."

The problem is that the internet is part of the entire world, where those practices have a different force and meaning.

"The world was not ready for the explosion of the internet from a bunch of small communities to something we all use," Mr. Bogost said. Besides the trolls exporting their behavior, he notes, "there's something about the internet that makes lots of us go too far — a customer complaint on Twitter usually sounds like the worst thing ever."

That tendency to overdo it became visible as the worst kind of trolling on the internet about a decade ago, when griefers exported their habits from the gaming world into the larger world. One typical gathering place to plan and launch group attacks was the site 4chan, where "anything goes" is the norm.

Griefers would go into virtual worlds like Second Life and cause trouble, like blocking imaginary hotel exits so players couldn't move from one place to another, or interrupting sessions in which people were interacting through their virtual characters.

From there, attacking people head-on — though almost always cloaked in anonymity — wasn't a big leap. And so much more on the internet became like a game, only the score consisted of attention, outrage or approval from like-minded trolls.

In 2012, Time magazine asked readers to vote online for Person of the Year. Thanks to trolls on 4chan, the North Korean leader, Kim Jong-un, began to pull ahead, though the poll was not binding and the magazine eventually chose President Obama.

It was little more than an irreverent stunt. When Mr. Kim was disallowed, however, the trolls hacked the site and inserted a code that distorted the results. The final list arranged the winners by their first letters, vertically spelling out "KJU GAS CHAMBERS."

Bad habits tend to worsen as those engaged in them get diminishing returns from their efforts and must become more outrageous to be noticed. And so trolling has become broader and more personal.

Anil Dash, an internet entrepreneur and activist who has been trolled for his outspoken comments about GamerGate, has made a study of his antagonists. He says trolling still has elements of its gaming roots, amplified by social media, where attention of any sort is viewed as winning.

"Online culture rewards engagement with points and likes, and it doesn't differentiate if what you are doing is scathing," he said. "Once a target is identified, it becomes a competition to see who can be the most ruthless, and the ones who feel the most powerless will do the most extreme thing just to get noticed and voted up."

Mr. Dash, who now sets aside time to monitor whether he is about to be attacked, has also seen others' personal information put online for others to exploit. Called doxing, this practice creates a sense of perpetual anxiety, he said, since it outlives the attacks.

He has also published essays on how to end abusive online behavior, and he blames the biggest internet companies for not better policing what people do online.

"You only need a list of about 1,000 words, and if one of them shows up, maybe something bad is happening," he said. "You can identify people who get a lot of retweets in the middle of these things. They are probably instigators. Bullying is programmatically easy to identify."

Besides Twitter, he said, YouTube comments and some parts of the user-generated news site Reddit could change the environment by using a combination of new algorithms and human editors. (Comments on articles in The New York Times are overseen by human editors.)

It's enough to make a bot give up, though apparently not Tay. In a blog post after Tay's griefing, Peter Lee, the vice president of Microsoft Research, vowed to "work toward contributing to an internet that represents the best, not the worst, of humanity."

A company spokesman said that artificial intelligence researchers had gone back to the drawing board with other experts from the company, including people from Xbox, who have dealt with griefers for years.

Why Some Men Don't Work: Video Games Have Gotten Really Good

BY QUOCTRUNG BUI | JULY 3, 2017

IF INNOVATIONS IN housework helped free women to enter the labor force in the 1960s and 1970s, could innovations in leisure — like League of Legends — be taking men out of the labor force today?

That's the logic behind a new working paper released on Monday by the National Bureau of Economic Research. The paper — by the economists Erik Hurst, Mark Aguiar, Mark Bils and Kerwin Charles — argues that video games help explain why younger men are working fewer hours.

That claim got a lot of attention last year when the University of Chicago published a graduation speech given by Mr. Hurst at its business school, where he discussed some of his preliminary findings. He says the paper is now ready to be read by the public.

By 2015, American men 31 to 55 were working about 163 fewer hours a year than that same age group did in 2000. Men 21 to 30 were working 203 fewer hours a year. One puzzle is why the working hours for young men fell so much more than those of their older counterparts. The gap between the two groups grew by about 40 hours a year, or a full workweek on average.

Other experts have pointed to a host of reasons — globalization, technological change, the shift to service work — that employers may not be hiring young men. Instead of looking at why employers don't want young men, this group of economists considered a different question: Why don't young men want to work?

Mr. Hurst and his colleagues estimate that, since 2004, video games have been responsible for reducing the amount of work that young men do by 15 to 30 hours over the course of a year. Using the recession as a natural experiment, the authors studied how people who suddenly

STRUGGLES IN GAMING COMMUNITIES **193**

found themselves with extra time spent their leisure hours, then estimated how increases in video game time affected work.

Between 2004 and 2015, young men's leisure time grew by 2.3 hours a week. A majority of that increase — 60 percent — was spent playing video games, according to government time use surveys. In contrast, young women's leisure time grew by 1.4 hours a week. A negligible amount of that extra time was spent on video games. Likewise for older men and older women: Neither group reported having spent any meaningful extra free time playing video games.

The analysis excluded full-time students, and showed that the amount of time young men spent on household chores or child care was not going up.

In some ways, the increase in video game time for men makes sense: Median wages for men have been stagnant for decades. Over the same period, the quality of video games has grown significantly. In the 1990s, games like Mario Bros. were little more than eight-bit virtual toys. Today, you and your closest buddies can go on quests in games like World of Warcraft that can last for days.

Large, social video games did not become hugely popular until the release of World of Warcraft in late 2004. These games are very different from more rudimentary games like Pong and Space Invaders that older men grew up playing.

Experts say that the social aspect is particularly important.

"Games provide a sense of waking in the morning with one goal: I'm trying to improve this skill, teammates are counting on me, and my online community is relying on me," said Jane McGonigal, a video game scholar and game designer. "There is a routine and daily progress that does a good job at replacing traditional work."

Adam Alter, a professor of marketing and psychology at New York University who studies digital addiction, highlighted the fact that, unlike TV shows or concerts, today's video games don't end.

Most forms of entertainment have some form of a stopping cue — signals that remind you that a certain act or episode is ending, like a commercial or a timer. "Many video games don't have them," Mr. Alter said. "They're built to be endless or have long-range goals that we don't like to abandon."

These characteristics make video games attractive to many people, and 41 percent of the American game-playing population are women, according to the video gaming advocacy group Entertainment Software Association. But this data showed no increase in video game time for women.

Mr. Hurst argues that women are more likely to choose the types of mobile games that people tend to play while doing something else, like riding in a car or standing in line. The time use survey captures only people's primary activity, not the secondary nature of casual mobile games like Candy Crush.

The analysis also did not count activities like using Facebook and Snapchat or browsing the web. Time spent on those activities did not grow as much as time spent on video games.

Some economists are skeptical of the conclusions, pointing out that the labor force participation rates for young men in other countries where video games are popular, like Japan, have not fallen in similar fashion.

But if we accept the authors' claim that some segment of men is dropping out of the labor force to play games, is that necessarily a bad thing?

Young non-college-educated men — the group most likely to be home playing games — are more likely to say that they are happy than similar men a decade ago. Older non-college-educated men are the unhappier ones.

According to Mr. Hurst, young men may simply be shuffling around the years in their life that they want to work. "Why not have a little fun in your 20s and work in your 80s?" he said.

Of course, that assumes that young Americans who choose video games over work — a group for whom there is no historical data — will be able to find good jobs someday. And that they won't be seduced by the kinds of games available in 2070.

The Real Problem With Video Games

OPINION | BY SETH SCHIESEL | MARCH 13, 2018

DONALD TRUMP has long claimed that exposure to simulated violence in video games begets violent tendencies in real life. "Video game violence and glorification must be stopped — it is creating monsters!" he tweeted in 2012.

In the wake of the school shooting in Parkland, Fla., as the nation debated gun control, Mr. Trump returned to that theme. "We have to look at the internet because a lot of bad things are happening to young kids and young minds, and their minds are being formed," he said. He went on to implicate video games in particular: "I'm hearing more and more people say the level of violence on video games is really shaping young people's thoughts."

On Thursday, President Trump summoned video game executives to the White House to castigate them for the violence depicted in their products. The executives were joined by Republican members of Congress and by activists who have campaigned against violence in media.

The White House meeting did not, however, include any social scientists who have studied the effects of video games. That would have been too problematic. Decades of research, after all, have failed to find any significant relationship between playing violent video games and behaving violently in real life.

If anything, there may be a stronger connection between school violence and the sort of creative writing educators seek to foster. When the United States Secret Service and the Department of Education studied violence in schools, they found that 37 percent of attackers "exhibited an interest in violence in their own writings, such as poems, essays, or journal entries," while only 12 percent exhibited an interest in violent video games.

Video games do not create murderers. With his Thursday meeting, the president was merely engaging in political distraction.

And yet Mr. Trump was absolutely right when he said that "bad things" are happening on the internet. Video games do have a big problem, but it is not stylized virtual violence. Rather, it is the bigotry, social abuse, sexism and other toxic behavior to which players too often subject one another when gaming together online.

In other words: It's not the content; it's the culture.

Listen to the voice communications of almost any popular online first-person shooter game and you will hear players constantly using racial and homophobic slurs. Make a mistake in just about any team-based combat game and it won't be long before one of your teammates chastises you with some vile epithet. There is more than one game community where "Jew" is used as a verb, meaning to make money. In many games, women who speak up on voice communications are routinely mocked and harassed.

While researchers have devoted ample time to studying the emotional and psychological effects of virtual video game violence, the actual social behavior of players has largely escaped academic attention. That should change. The racism, homophobia and misogyny prevalent in many online game precincts can amount to emotional abuse. This is a phenomenon that needs to be better understood and more widely known.

In this respect, Melania Trump's campaign against cyberbullying, largely rhetorical though it is, addresses a more serious problem than does her husband's concern with virtual gunplay. But there is not much the government can do about this.

Game companies, too, cannot be expected to constantly police the communications and communities of millions of players. Some companies, such as Blizzard Entertainment (the creator of "World of Warcraft") and Riot Games ("League of Legends"), deserve credit for at least attempting to curb the toxicity of their customers, allowing conscientious players to report their obnoxious peers and then devoting personnel to reviewing complaints and disciplining consistently abusive players. But it is a gargantuan task.

As with many cultural crises, it is up to everyday people, not politicians or executives, to generate true solutions. The real responsibility lies with the players themselves — and for younger players, to their parents as well — to confront the real problem with video games.

SETH SCHIESEL is a former reporter and video game critic for The New York Times.

Video Game Addiction Tries to Move From Basement to Doctor's Office

BY TIFFANY HSU | JUNE 17, 2018

VIDEO GAMES WORK HARD to hook players. Designers use predictive algorithms and principles of behavioral economics to keep fans engaged. When new games are reviewed, the most flattering accolade might be "I can't put it down."

Now, the World Health Organization is saying players can actually become addicted.

On Monday, "gaming disorder" will appear in a new draft of the organization's International Classification of Diseases, the highly regarded compendium of medical conditions.

Concerns about the influence of video games are dovetailing with increasing scrutiny over the harmful aspects of technology, as consumers look for ways to scale back consumption of social media and online entertainment.

The W.H.O. designation may help legitimize worries about video game fans who neglect other parts of their lives. It could also make gamers more willing to seek treatment, encourage more therapists to provide it and increase the chances that insurance companies would cover it.

"It's going to untie our hands in terms of treatment, in that we'll be able to treat patients and get reimbursed," said Dr. Petros Levounis, the chairman of the psychiatry department at Rutgers New Jersey Medical School. "We won't have to go dancing around the issue, calling it depression or anxiety or some other consequence of the issue but not the issue itself."

Around the world, 2.6 billion people play video games, including two-thirds of American households, according to the Entertainment Software Association. Annual revenue for the industry is expected to grow 31 percent to $180.1 billion globally within three years. Fortnite — the latest blockbuster, in which players battle to be the last one

The study center at the Serenity Mountain adolescent treatment branch of the ReStart internet and video game addiction center in Monroe, Wash.

standing in an apocalyptic storm — recently earned a reported $300 million in a month.

The industry has pushed back against the W.H.O. classification, which is expected to be formally adopted next year, calling it "deeply flawed" while pointing to the "educational, therapeutic and recreational value of games."

But gaming has long had an addictive quality. The game Ever-Quest, introduced nearly 20 years ago, was nicknamed EverCrack for the long binges it inspired.

Now, mental health professionals say they increasingly see players who have lost control.

"I have patients who come in suffering from an addiction to Candy Crush Saga, and they're substantially similar to people who come in with a cocaine disorder," Dr. Levounis said. "Their lives are ruined, their interpersonal relationships suffer, their physical condition suffers."

Sand tray therapy, a hands-on therapeutic technique, in the art room at Serenity Mountain. Some mental health professionals see gaming addiction as a symptom or a side effect of more familiar conditions, such as depression or anxiety.

Although gaming addiction treatment is starting to draw more attention, there is little insurance coverage or accreditation for specialists to treat it. Wilderness camps and rehabilitation centers have sprung up, but can cost tens of thousands of dollars, with scarce proof of success. Mental health generalists are trying to apply familiar therapies for anxiety or alcoholism to patients with an uncontrollable craving for, say, World of Warcraft.

Players seeking help often cannot find it.

Kim DeVries, a gift shop owner in Tucson, said she started looking for a gaming addiction specialist two years ago after her son failed out of college and was struggling to hold a job.

Ms. DeVries wanted someone who understood her son's seeming compulsion to gaze into a glowing screen for 16 hours on some days, subsisting on crackers and pita chips and listening on a headset to strangers discussing strategy for League of Legends.

She struck out. "They didn't exist — there was just no such thing," she said.

Ms. DeVries now resorts to forbidding her son, 24, to play games after 11 p.m.

"At times, I'll walk by and hear the tap-tapping on his keyboard, and it'll make me shudder," she said. Her son declined to be interviewed.

The video game industry is expanding so quickly that medical research has struggled to keep up.

An early study — published in 2009 — found that nearly 9 percent of young players were addicted to their games. Many experts believe that the number has increased as games have become more advanced, more social and more mobile, putting them as close as the smartphone in your purse or pocket.

"There's a massive tsunami coming that we're not prepared for," said Cam Adair, the founder of Game Quitters, an online support community.

But some mental health professionals insist that gaming disorder is not a stand-alone medical condition. Rather, they see it as a symptom or a side effect of more familiar conditions, such as depression or anxiety.

"We don't know how to treat gaming disorder," said Nancy Petry, a psychology professor and addiction expert with the University of Connecticut. "It's such a new condition and phenomenon."

In Asia, a center of video game activity and addiction, rehabilitation centers designed to stamp out uncontrollable playing have existed for years. South Korea bars young players from online gaming portals between midnight and 6 a.m. and subsidizes some gaming addiction treatment clinics.

But in the United States, getting care is often an exercise in frustration.

Many parents and patients rely on Google and word of mouth. In forums like StopGaming, struggling players complain about being laughed at by psychiatrists. No formal organization exists to set treatment standards and answer questions, experts said.

The grounds of ReStart at Serenity Mountain. The gaming industry has pushed back against the World Health Organization's classification of "gaming disorder."

"It's very wild, wild West," Mr. Adair said. "There's no consistent quality control."

As a teenager, depressed and anxious after being bullied, Mr. Adair dropped out of school and began fixating on games like StarCraft in his parents' basement in Calgary, Alberta, he said.

He told his parents that he had a job, but would sneak back home to play. At 19, he said, he considered taking his life, eventually writing a suicide note.

When Mr. Adair tried to find help, he found few resources.

He wrote about his struggles online and later delivered a popular TEDx talk. Game Quitters, the online forum he started, now draws 50,000 participants a month from 91 countries. It suggests programming, yoga and other activities to replace gaming.

Another resource, the On-Line Gamers Anonymous forum, was founded by Liz Woolley in 2002 after her son, an avid gamer, committed suicide. She maintains a list of medical professionals on the site. But she said she was not always able to confirm how much experience they had with gaming addiction.

"Any type of treatment is better than nothing," Ms. Woolley said. "At least we have somewhere to send people other than to their basement."

Another kind of obsessive disorder may provide a template, and a warning, for activists seeking more support and research into gaming addiction: Compulsive gambling was first recognized by the World Health Organization and the American Psychiatric Association more than three decades ago.

Formal recognition from medical organizations helps "bring everybody to the table," said Keith S. Whyte, the executive director of the National Council on Problem Gambling. Next month, his group will host its 32nd national conference.

But inclusion is "not a magic bullet," Mr. Whyte said. A "complex patchwork" of national and state certifications for gambling addiction made it easier for some insurers to deny reimbursement, he said.

"You still have to do a tremendous amount of advocacy," he said.

Although reliable treatment for gaming addiction can be hard to find, demand is high.

A residential recovery program near Seattle, ReStart, charges adult patients nearly $30,000 for the first seven weeks of care. It has a monthslong waiting list.

Six patients, usually men, are initially placed at a rural retreat and weaned off electronics while being taught how to socialize and exercise. ReStart, which is nearly a decade old, started a program for adolescents last year.

Hilarie Cash, a co-founder, said she was working to develop a certification program for addiction disorders including internet and gaming dependency. When she speaks at mental health conferences, she said, she often sees counselors "taking notes like mad."

Addiction therapists are "getting called more often" about gaming disorder, Dr. Cash said, and many are "kind of tacking it onto what they already offer."

"They're trying to learn as best they can," she said.

Endless Gaming May Be a Bad Habit. That Doesn't Make It a Mental Illness.

BY BENEDICT CAREY | JULY 2, 2018

The World Health Organization has made "internet gaming" a diagnosable disorder. But many experts aren't even sure it exists.

THE WORLD HEALTH ORGANIZATION last month added "internet gaming disorder" to its manual of psychiatric diagnoses, and the reaction was, shall we say, muted.

At a time when millions of grown adults exchange one-liners with Siri or Alexa, the diagnosis seems years overdue, doesn't it?

Put down your phone and look around: If half the people you see walking down the street or riding the bus with you are face-deep in a small screen, then it's not a wild leap to think that some percentage of us, particularly those younger and male, have fallen hard for "Fortnite" or "League of Legends" or "World of Warcraft" and cannot get up, except to fetch the occasional bowl of Lucky Charms.

They're stuck. They sleep with their heads on keyboards. They could use a friend of the breathing, let's-go-to-the-park variety. They could use some help.

Yet embracing I.G.D., as it's known, as a new mental health disorder has its own perils. Many psychologists are skeptical that it exists at all as a stand-alone problem. The diagnostic criteria are still fuzzy, and the potential for overdiagnosis is enormous.

I.G.D. is a case study in what happens when researchers become convinced that a bad habit has become something different: a disorder. The studies pile up and the notion takes on a life of its own — one that may or may not be persuasive to putative "patients."

"The question is, what's the difference between a bad habit and a disorder, and where do you draw that line," said Scott Lilienfeld, a professor of psychology at Emory University.

"Some, like me, believe there's often no reliable way to do that. Others disagree. The point is, you need to be very careful in doing so" for people who need help to buy in.

The W.H.O.'s definition of gaming disorder is a mouthful:

A pattern of gaming behavior characterized by impaired control over gaming, increasing priority given to gaming over other activities to the extent that gaming takes precedence over other interests and daily activities, and continuation or escalation of gaming despite the occurrence of negative consequences.

As a diagnosis, it's a potential blockbuster. Estimates of its prevalence — up to 9 percent of all gamers — mean that tens of millions of mostly young people worldwide may now be said to have a mental disorder.

Some of them surely do, whatever its underlying dynamics.

"The kids I see truly have a problem, and it has disastrous effects on many parts of their lives — school performance, social life, their

DANIEL ZENDER

moods," said Dr. Clifford Sussman, a psychiatrist in Washington who treats compulsive gaming with psychotherapy.

"It doesn't much matter what you call it, the point is to give them tools" to control the habit, he added, and better integrate it into their lives.

Many other psychiatrists agree and say they have treated the compulsion successfully. But the American Psychological Association, among other groups, takes exception to the diagnosis.

The association argues that the definition remains too vague, and that mood problems may in fact precede excessive gaming, not vice versa. The new label reflects a "moral panic," the critics say — an unfounded fear of new technology that years ago had parents and some experts finger-wagging about the mentally corrosive effects of TV, and before that, radio.

"There's a kernel of truth in what the partisans are saying," said Christopher Ferguson, a psychologist at Stetson University who has been a skeptic of the many ills attributed to gaming. "There's something to this, although we really don't know enough to understand it entirely."

Parts of the published science thus far, he said, have not been reassuring. Take, for example, the search for a "signature" of the disorder in the brain.

In one recent study, a group of scientists in China and Europe asked 38 people they identified as having I.G.D. to put their heads inside an MRI scanner.

Compared to peers who had less compulsive gaming habits, the I.G.D. group "showed significantly decreased cortical thickness in the left lateral orbitofrontal cortex, inferior parietal lobule, bilateral cuneus, precentral gyrus, and right middle temporal gyrus," the researchers announced.

Another report, also using brain imaging, concluded that people with I.G.D. had "decreased connectivity between the left amygdala and left middle frontal and precentral gyrus."

That's a lot of fancy-sounding brain regions. But the conclusions are all virtually meaningless, since no one knows much about how those regions interact, or why one gamer's bilateral cuneus happens to be thicker than another's.

Another recent study focused on treatment: not just any treatment but bupropion, an antidepressant often used in smoking cessation.

The study found that, after 12 weeks, "depressive symptoms, attention and impulsivity improved," and so did scores, for some, on something called the Young Internet Addiction Scale.

No word on whether participants in the study actually learned to manage their gaming habits in a lasting way.

"Once you decide there's a disorder, you start looking for it in people's brains and trying to knock it out, like you would a brain tumor," Dr. Lilienfeld said.

But of course there is no tumor in this case.

Finally, yet another recent study hinted that one way to break the gaming trance is to put screen junkies on horseback.

After seven days of "equine-assisted activities and therapies," a group of adolescents diagnosed with I.G.D. showed improvement in "avoidance and anxiety scores," this study concluded.

Horse riding, usually with a therapist-guide riding alongside, giving instruction and encouragement, has shown some benefit for people with autism, traumatic brain injury and post-traumatic stress.

Now…gamers.

Whether W.H.O.'s inclusion of compulsive gaming eventually leads to better research, or to standardized treatments that reliably change behavior, is an open question.

But for now it would be hard to blame anyone with a serious joystick jones for balking at the prospect of a "disorder."

A bad habit may be bad. But at least fixing it doesn't involve brain scans, antidepressant pills or clinging for dear life to some cantering Cheyenne or Misty.

The digital horses are a lot safer to ride, after all. And you get to carry a sword.

Glossary

augmented reality Technology that overlays digital content over a view of the real world, used in some video games.

avatar A virtual character representing the player, often customized to their tastes.

console Traditional video game platform, like PlayStation or Nintendo.

consumerism Orienting one's lifestyle around purchasing goods and services.

doxing Harassing an individual by finding and exposing their personal information.

emergent behavior Game playing techniques not anticipated by a designer.

esports Competitive video game playing.

freemium A free web service that makes its profit from additional in-app or in-game purchases.

game mechanics The rules that determine how a game is played, including the physics and allowed combinations of moves.

gamer A person who plays video games frequently.

gaming disorder The technical term for the diagnosis of addiction to playing video games.

graphics Images generated by computer, the visual component of video games.

hack A solution to a problem that is often creative and ad hoc, often applying to computers.

hyperlink A link from a file or document to another file, usually represented with a bolded or highlighted word.

influencer An individual whose authority to influence purchases or public opinion derives from their online following.

in-game currency Virtual currency used within a game, which can be acquired through in-game activities or purchases.

LAN party A social gathering based on a local area network of computers, often for the purpose of playing games.

massively multiplayer online game An online video game with a large number of players on the same server.

misogyny Hostility to or hatred of women, a common issue in video game communities.

mobile game A game designed for handheld devices, rather than traditional consoles.

neophyte A person who is new to a community, practice, or subject matter.

screen time The amount of time an individual spends on their computer or other device.

sedentary The tendency to remain seated or inactive for long periods of time.

shooter A style of game in which players' primary activity is shooting enemies.

streaming The continuous flow of audio or video while the user watches or listens, often used for video game broadcasts.

tablet Handheld device with a touchscreen, often used in mobile games.

trauma An extremely hurtful experience that often remains in someone's memory.

trolling The practice of provoking people online by making inflammatory comments.

Media Literacy Terms

"Media literacy" refers to the ability to access, understand, critically assess and create media. The following terms are important components of media literacy, and they will help you critically engage with the articles in this title.

angle The aspect of a news story that a journalist focuses on and develops.

attribution The method by which a source is identified or by which facts and information are assigned to the person who provided them.

balance Principle of journalism that both perspectives of an argument should be presented in a fair way.

bias A disposition of prejudice in favor of a certain idea, person, or perspective.

byline Name of the writer, usually placed between the headline and the story.

caption Identifying copy for a picture; also called a legend or cutline.

chronological order Method of writing a story presenting the details of the story in the order in which they occurred.

commentary A type of story that is an expression of opinion on recent events by a journalist generally known as a commentator.

credibility The quality of being trustworthy and believable, said of a journalistic source.

editorial Article of opinion or interpretation.

feature story Article designed to entertain as well as to inform.

headline Type, usually 18 point or larger, used to introduce a story.

human interest story Type of story that focuses on individuals and how events or issues affect their life, generally offering a sense of relatability to the reader.

impartiality Principle of journalism that a story should not reflect a journalist's bias and should contain balance.

intention The motive or reason behind something, such as the publication of a news story.

interview story Type of story in which the facts are gathered primarily by interviewing another person or persons.

inverted pyramid Method of writing a story using facts in order of importance, beginning with a lead and then gradually adding paragraphs in order of relevance from most interesting to least interesting.

motive The reason behind something, such as the publication of a news story or a source's perspective on an issue.

news story An article or style of expository writing that reports news, generally in a straightforward fashion and without editorial comment.

op-ed An opinion piece that reflects a prominent individual's opinion on a topic of interest.

paraphrase The summary of an individual's words, with attribution, rather than a direct quotation of their exact words.

plagiarism An attempt to pass another person's work as one's own without attribution.

quotation The use of an individual's exact words indicated by the use of quotation marks and proper attribution.

reliability The quality of being dependable and accurate, said of a journalistic source.

rhetorical device Technique in writing intending to persuade the reader or communicate a message from a certain perspective.

source The origin of the information reported in journalism.

sports reporting A type of story that reports on sporting events or topics related to sports.

style A distinctive use of language in writing or speech; also a news or publishing organization's rules for consistent use of language with regards to spelling, punctuation, typography and capitalization, usually regimented by a house style guide.

tone A manner of expression in writing or speech.

Media Literacy Questions

1. Steven Zeitchik's article "Go to the Mattresses (No, It's Not a Mob War)" (page 10) is a human interest story. How does this article capture the spirit of early online gaming communities?

2. Diane Mehta's article "Four Hours of Screen Time? No Problem" (page 30) is an op-ed. What perspective does Mehta offer, and why is it relevant to her subject of child video game usage?

3. Clive Thompson's article "The Minecraft Generation" (page 47) is a feature story. What is the core theme of Minecraft as Thompson explores it, and how does he convey that theme?

4. What is the angle of Hayley Krischer's article "Closing the Gender Gap, One E-Battle at a Time" (page 66)? How does her interview subject help explore that angle?

5. Michael J. de la Merced and Nick Wingfield's article "Bobby Kotick's Activision Blizzard to Buy King Digital, Maker of Candy Crush" (page 89) uses the inverted pyramid format, where the most important information is presented first. Compare the first and last paragraphs. How did the authors decide which information to prioritize?

6. Pay close attention to the descriptive language of Amy Butcher's op-ed "Pokémon Go See the World in Its Splendor" (page 93). What rhetorical devices does she use? What tone does that create?

7. Seth Schiesel's article "The Land of the Video Geek" (page 113) is a human interest story about early e-athletes in South Korea. Compare it with Steven Zeitchik's article, "Go to the Mattresses (No, It's Not a Mob War)" (page 10). What are the similarities and differences in how they convey their subject matter? To what audience is each article meant to appeal?

8. Alan Feuer's article "Seeking to Be Both N.F.L. and ESPN of Video Gaming" (page 126) depicts the rise to prominence of the American company Major League Gaming. How does the headline convey the core themes of the story? Does it leave anything out?

9. Identify the sources used in Gregory Schmidt's article "Esports Sees Profit in Attracting Female Gamers" (page 141). What makes these sources reliable, and what perspectives do they offer? How does the author attribute these sources?

10. What is the intention of Daniel E. Slotnik's article "Gamer's Death Pushes Risks of Live Streaming Into View" (page 148)? How do the issues discussed in the essay inform that intention?

11. Nick Wingfield's article "Feminist Critics of Video Games Facing Threats in 'GamerGate' Campaign" (page 165) describes a controversial topic and a climate of harassment amidst that controversy. How does Wingfield maintain the journalistic principle of balance in his account?

12. Quoctrung Bui's article "Why Some Men Don't Work: Video Games Have Gotten Really Good" (page 193) relies on a combination of sources: statistical data, direct quotation and paraphrase. How do each of these sources contribute to the broader story Bui tells?

Citations

All citations in this list are formatted according to the Modern Language Association's (MLA) style guide.

BOOK CITATION

THE NEW YORK TIMES EDITORIAL STAFF. *Online Gaming: The Surge in Esports and Mobile Gaming.* New York: New York Times Educational Publishing, 2019.

ONLINE ARTICLE CITATIONS

BILTON, NICK. "Disruptions: Minecraft, an Obsession and an Educational Tool." *The New York Times*, 15 Sept. 2013, https://bits.blogs.nytimes.com/2013/09/15/minecraft-an-obsession-and-an-educational-tool/.

BOSS, SHIRA. "Even in a Virtual World, 'Stuff' Matters." *The New York Times*, 9 Sept. 2007, https://www.nytimes.com/2007/09/09/business/yourmoney/09second.html.

BOWLES, NELLIE. "All We Want to Do Is Watch Each Other Play Video Games." *The New York Times*, 2 May 2018, https://www.nytimes.com/2018/05/02/style/fortnite.html.

BRAY, CHAD. "An Angry Birds Empire: Games, Toys, Movies and Now an I.P.O." *The New York Times*, 5 Sept. 2017, https://www.nytimes.com/2017/09/05/business/dealbook/angry-birds-rovio-ipo.html.

BUI, QUOCTRUNG. "Why Some Men Don't Work: Video Games Have Gotten Really Good." *The New York Times*, 3 July 2017, https://www.nytimes.com/2017/07/03/upshot/why-some-men-dont-work-video-games-have-gotten-really-good.html.

BUTCHER, AMY. "Pokemon Go See the World in Its Splendor." *The New York Times*, 14 July 2016, https://www.nytimes.com/2016/07/17/opinion/sunday/pokemon-go-see-the-world-in-its-splendor.html.

CAREY, BENEDICT. "Endless Gaming May Be a Bad Habit. That Doesn't Make

It a Mental Illness." *The New York Times*, 2 July 2018, https://www.nytimes
.com/2018/07/02/health/internet-gaming-addiction.html.

DE LA MERCED, MICHAEL J., AND NICK WINGFIELD. "Bobby Kotick's Activision
Blizzard to Buy King Digital, Maker of Candy Crush." *The New York Times*,
2 Nov. 2015, https://www.nytimes.com/2015/11/03/business/dealbook
/activision-blizzardto-buy-king-digital-maker-of-candy-crush.html.

FEUER, ALAN. "Seeking to Be Both N.F.L. and ESPN of Video Gaming." *The
New York Times*, 9 Aug. 2013, https://www.nytimes.com/2013/08/11
/nyregion/seeking-to-be-both-nfl-and-espn-of-video-gaming.html.

GARCIA, SANDRA E. "A Non-Gamer's Guide to Fortnite, the Game That Conquered All the Screens." *The New York Times*, 25 July 2018, https://www
.nytimes.com/2018/07/25/arts/what-is-fortnite-battle-royale-nyt.html.

HARDY, QUENTIN. "How Gaming Helped Launch the Attack of the Internet
Trolls." *The New York Times*, 8 June 2016, https://www.nytimes.com
/2016/06/09/technology/how-gaming-helped-launch-the-attack-of-the
-internet-trolls.html.

HELFT, MIGUEL. "Will Zynga Become the Google of Games?" *The New York
Times*, 24 July 2010, https://www.nytimes.com/2010/07/25/business
/25zynga.html.

HERRMAN, JOHN. "With Twitch, Amazon Tightens Grip on Live Streams of Video Games." *The New York Times*, 17 June 2018, https://www.nytimes
.com/2018/06/17/business/media/amazon-twitch-video-games.html.

HUDSON, LAURA. "Twine, the Video-Game Technology for All." *The New York
Times*, 19 Nov. 2014, https://www.nytimes.com/2014/11/23/magazine
/twine-the-video-game-technology-for-all.html.

ITO, ROBERT. "In 'GTFO,' Female Video Gamers Fight Back." *The New York
Times*, 6 Mar. 2015, https://www.nytimes.com/2015/03/08/movies
/in-the-documentary-gtfo-female-video-gamers-fight-back.html.

KAN, KAROLINE, AND AUSTIN RAMZY. "China Embraces a Game About a
Traveling Frog." *The New York Times*, 26 Jan. 2018, https://www.nytimes
.com/2018/01/26/world/asia/china-travel-frog-game.html.

KRISCHER, HAYLEY. "Closing the Gender Gap, One E-Battle at a Time." *The
New York Times*, 24 June 2016, https://www.nytimes.com/2016/06/26
/fashion/league-of-legends-women-video-games.html.

MEHTA, DIANE. "Four Hours of Screen Time? No Problem." *The New York
Times*, 16 Nov. 2012, https://parenting.blogs.nytimes.com/2012/11/16
/four-hours-of-screen-time-no-problem/.

NIEVA, RICHARD. "Video Gaming on the Pro Tour, for Glory but Little Gold." *The New York Times*, 28 Nov. 2012, https://www.nytimes.com/2012/11/29 /technology/personaltech/video-gaming-on-the-pro-tour-for-glory-but -little-gold.html.

ROSENBLOOM, STEPHANIE. "It's Love at First Kill." *The New York Times*, 22 Apr. 2011, https://www.nytimes.com/2011/04/24/fashion/24avatar.html.

SARKEESIAN, ANITA. "It's Game Over for 'Gamers.' " *The New York Times*, 28 Oct. 2014, https://www.nytimes.com/2014/10/29/opinion/anita -sarkeesian-on-video-games-great-future.html.

SCHIESEL, SETH. "The Land of the Video Geek." *The New York Times*, 8 Oct. 2006, https://www.nytimes.com/2006/10/08/arts/08schi.html.

SCHIESEL, SETH. "The Real Problem With Video Games." *The New York Times*, 13 Mar. 2018, https://www.nytimes.com/2018/03/13/opinion /video-games-toxic-violence.html.

SCHILLINGER, LIESL. "How I Became Addicted to Online Word Games." *The New York Times*, 18 Mar. 2017, https://www.nytimes.com/2017/03/18/style /addicted-to-online-games-words-with-friends-prolific.html.

SCHMIDT, GREGORY. "Esports Sees Profit in Attracting Female Gamers." *The New York Times*, 21 Dec. 2016, https://www.nytimes.com/2016/12/21 /technology/personaltech/video-game-makers-try-to-get-better-at -luring-women-to-esports.html.

SCOTT, MARK. "Executive at Struggling Rovio, Maker of Angry Birds, Pushes Silver Lining." *The New York Times*, 2 Sept. 2015, https://bits.blogs.nytimes .com/2015/09/02/executive-at-struggling-rovio-maker-of-angry-birds -pushes-silver-lining/.

SEGAL, DAVID. "Behind League of Legends, E-Sports' Main Attraction." *The New York Times*, 10 Oct. 2014, https://www.nytimes.com/2014/10/12 /technology/riot-games-league-of-legends-main-attraction-esports.html.

SLOTNIK, DANIEL E. "Gamer's Death Pushes Risks of Live Streaming Into View." *The New York Times*, 15 Mar. 2017, https://www.nytimes.com/2017/03/15 /technology/personaltech/live-streaming-gaming-death.html.

THOMPSON, CLIVE. "The Minecraft Generation." *The New York Times*, 15 Apr. 2016, https://www.nytimes.com/2016/04/17/magazine/the-minecraft -generation.html.

TRACY, MARC. "Big Ten Universities Entering a New Realm: E-Sports." *The New York Times*, 19 Jan. 2017, https://www.nytimes.com/2017/01/19/sports /big-ten-is-entering-a-new-realm-e-sports.html.

TSU, TIFFANY. "Video Game Addiction Tries to Move from Basement to the Doctor's Office." *The New York Times*, 17 June 2018, https://www.nytimes.com/2018/06/17/business/video-game-addiction.html.

VICTOR, DANIEL. "Candy Crush and the Curve of Impressiveness." *The New York Times*, 12 Mar. 2014, https://bits.blogs.nytimes.com/2014/03/12/candy-crush-and-the-curve-of-impressiveness/.

WINGFIELD, NICK. "Activision Buys Major League Gaming to Broaden Role in E-Sports." *The New York Times*, 4 Jan. 2016, https://www.nytimes.com/2016/01/05/technology/activision-buys-major-league-gaming-to-broaden-role-in-e-sports.html.

WINGFIELD, NICK. "Feminist Critics of Video Games Facing Threats in 'GamerGate' Campaign." *The New York Times*, 15 Oct. 2014, https://www.nytimes.com/2014/10/16/technology/gamergate-women-video-game-threats-anita-sarkeesian.html.

WINGFIELD, NICK. "From the Land of Angry Birds, a Mobile Game Maker Takes Off." *The New York Times*, 8 Oct. 2012, https://bits.blogs.nytimes.com/2012/10/08/from-the-land-of-angry-birds-a-mobile-game-maker-lifts-off/.

WINGFIELD, NICK. "A New Phase for World of Warcraft's Lead Designer: His Own Start-Up." *The New York Times*, 11 Sept. 2016, https://www.nytimes.com/2016/09/12/technology/a-new-phase-for-world-of-warcrafts-lead-designer-his-own-start-up.html.

WINGFIELD, NICK. "What's Twitch? Gamers Know, and Amazon Is Spending $1 Billion on It." *The New York Times*, 25 Aug. 2014, https://www.nytimes.com/2014/08/26/technology/amazon-nears-a-deal-for-twitch.html.

WINGFIELD, NICK, AND VINDU GOEL. "Mario, Nintendo's Mustachioed Gaming Legend, Arrives on iPhones." *The New York Times*, 14 Dec. 2016, https://www.nytimes.com/2016/12/14/technology/mario-nintendos-mustachioed-gaming-legend-arrives-on-iphones.html.

ZEITCHIK, STEVEN. "Go to the Mattresses (No, It's Not a Mob War)." *The New York Times*, 10 July 2005, https://www.nytimes.com/2005/07/10/nyregion/nyregionspecial2/go-to-the-mattresses-no-its-not-a-mob-war.html.

Index

A

Accel Partners, 83–84
Activision Blizzard, 8, 61, 69, 70–71, 89–92, 109, 117, 119, 136, 138–140, 167, 188, 198
Aguiar, Mark, 193
Alter, Adam, 194–195
Amazon, 74, 76, 82, 134–137, 139, 141, 148, 160–164
American Psychological Association, 208
Angry Birds, 8, 75, 83–84, 85, 87–88, 91, 107–110, 172
Anthropy, Anna, 178–179
Apax Partners, 92
Apple, 33, 48, 57, 81, 83, 84, 89, 98, 100, 111
Arhancet, Steve, 43
Au, Wagner James, 19

B

Baldwin, Adam, 168
Balsbaugh, Brian, 121
Beck, Brandon, 39, 40, 41, 43, 70
Beck, Dustin, 36, 39, 46
Begscape, 177–178
Benjamin, Walter, 49
Bergensten, Jens, 54
Bezos, Jeff, 134
Big Ten universities, esports and, 146–147
Bils, Mark, 193
Blevins, Tyler, 160, 164

Bloomfield, Robert J., 22
Bogost, Ian, 190, 191
Bonfire Studios, 69–70
Bornstein, Steve, 138
Bowman, Ben, 150

C

Callari, James, 10, 11, 13, 14
Call of Duty, 72, 90, 126, 128, 133, 134, 136, 138, 140, 156, 172, 185
Candy Crush, 8, 75, 85–86, 89–92, 107, 109, 195, 200
Cash, Hilarie, 204
Charles, Kerwin, 193
Clash of Clans, 71, 83, 109
Cole, David, 99
Cowan, David, 135

D

Dash, Anil, 191–192
Depression Quest, 173, 188
Destiny, 90
Dezuanni, Michael, 58
Dibbell, Julian, 18
DiGiovanni, Sundance, 122, 128, 129–130, 139
DiMassimo, Mark, 108
doxing, 192
Drake, 72, 153, 160
Dreunen, Joost van, 39, 99, 101
Duranske, Benjamin, 22, 23

E

Edwards, Kate, 169
Electronic Arts, 69, 78, 79, 91, 139, 167
Ellis, Kit, 99
Ellison, Cara, 180
Emmert, Jack, 190
Entertainment Software Association, 26, 167–168, 169, 178, 195, 199
Epic Games, 72
esports, 36–46, 66–68, 113–120, 121–125, 126–133, 134–137, 138–140, 141–145, 146–147, 152–159, 160–164
eSports Management Group, 121
Everquest, 7, 25
Everything You Swallow Will One Day Come Up Like a Stone, 183–184
Evil Geniuses, 122

F

Facebook, 34, 68, 75, 76, 77, 78, 81, 83, 84, 86, 109, 125, 160, 162–163, 195
Fanning, Colin, 49, 50
FarmVille, 75, 77, 78, 81, 82, 83, 86, 107, 109
Ferguson, Christopher, 208
Fitzpatrick, Catherine A., 20, 22
Fortnite, 7, 10, 72–74, 152, 153, 157, 160, 199, 206

Francois, Lester, 188
Frazzini, Mike, 136
freemium model, 87, 88, 89, 109
Frey, Seth, 61–62
Freytag, Brandon, 164
Froebel, Friedrich, 49

G
"GameLoading," 186, 188
Game Quitters, 202, 203
GamerGate, 9, 68, 165–169, 173, 185, 189, 191
GameSpot.com, 123
gaming addiction, 9, 165, 199–205
gaming disorder, 199, 202–205, 206–207
Garcia, Rob, 150–151
Garfield, Alexander, 122
George, Brent, 26
Google, 33, 48, 75, 76, 77, 81, 82, 125, 134, 139, 160, 161–162, 202
griefing, 60, 63, 189–192
"GTFO," 185–188

H
Halo, 64, 122, 139, 168
Haniver, Jenny, 185, 187
Harper, Greg, 84
Harvey, Stephanie, 143
Hawkins, Janine, 16, 20, 21, 22
Hed, Mikael, 109
Heitzmann, Rick, 78
Hit-Point, 111
Hoon Ju, 118
Howling Dogs, 175–178
Hurst, Erik, 193–195
Hyong Jun Hwang, 118

I
Ito, Mimi, 55–57, 65

J
Joseph, Barry, 62–63

K
Kan, Justin, 161
Kaplan, Daniel, 88
Katzenberg, Jeffrey, 77
Keighley, Geoff, 71
Kendall, Omar, 46
Kim Byung Kyu, 120
King Digital, 8, 85, 87, 88, 89–92, 107, 109
Klimas, Chris, 174
Klopfer, Eric, 35
Koster, Raph, 166
Kotick, Robert, 89–92, 138, 139, 140
Kowarski, Mike, 12, 14
Kuittinen, Tero, 108

L
LAN parties, 10–15
Lasky, Mitch, 40, 100
League of Legends, 7, 36–46, 66–68, 70, 135, 139, 146, 147, 152, 193, 198, 201, 206
Lee, Peter, 192
Lee Chung Gi, 117
Levin, Joel, 34
Levounis, Petros, 199, 200
Lilienfeld, Scott, 206–207, 209
Lim Yo-Hwan, 117, 118
Lin, Jeffrey, 45
Linden Lab, 18, 20
Lindsey, Patrick, 173
Locke, John, 49

M
Mafia Wars, 75
Major League Gaming, 121–122, 123, 126–133, 138–140

Mandel, Carrie, 21
Marino, Joe, 150
Mario, 69, 98–101, 194
McCarthy, Gregg, 14
McGonigal, Jane, 194
McInnes, Will, 110
McQuivey, James, 136
Merrill, Marc, 38, 39, 40, 41
Microsoft, 33, 48, 51, 52, 61, 64, 88, 91, 115, 119, 139, 160, 162, 171, 189, 192
Minecraft, 7, 33–35, 47–65, 72, 88, 91, 99
Mir, Rebecca, 49
Miyamoto, Shigeru, 69, 100
Mojang, 48, 50, 54, 56, 61, 64, 88
Molyneux, Peter, 50
Montessori, Maria, 49
Myers, Maddy, 187

N
Nelson, Randy, 100
Neon, Lydia, 179
Niantic, 100
Nintendo, 8–9, 69, 72, 74, 75, 84, 85, 98–101, 119, 144, 170, 171

O
On-line Gamers Anonymous, 203

P
Paananen, Ilkka, 84
Pardo, Rob, 69–71
Park Youngmok, 119
Persson, Markus, 33, 50–51, 52, 53, 54, 57
Pezzino, John, 11, 13, 15
Pincus, Mark, 75–82
Player 2, 179–180
Plott, Sean and Nick, 121, 124–125

Pokémon Go, 9, 93–97, 99–101
Porpentine, 175–178, 181–184
Pringle, Ramona, 25, 26, 27, 29
Prolific, 103–106
Puckett, Chris, 126, 131, 132–133

Q
Quinn, Zoe, 168, 173–174, 181, 185

R
Ratcliffe, Mitch, 19–20
Religioso, Mark, 141, 144, 145
ReStart, 200, 203, 204
Riccitiello, John, 69–70, 71
Riikola, Atte, 108
Riot Games, 36–46, 67, 70, 139, 146, 147, 198
Robinson, Anna Prosser, 143–144
Roblox, 30–32
Rovio, 8, 83, 84, 87–88, 91, 107–110

S
Sarkeesian, Anita, 165–169, 170–172
Schankler, Isaac, 173
Second Life, 7, 16–23, 102
Sepso, Mike, 129–130, 131, 132, 138–139
Shear, Emmett, 136–137, 161
Sherman, Michael, 146

Siciliano, Dan, 22
Skylanders, 90
Sorensen, Carl Theodor, 49
South Korea, 8, 36, 87, 113–120, 129, 140, 148, 202
StarCraft/StarCraft II, 39, 114, 115, 117, 119, 120, 121, 122, 124, 128, 129, 140, 203
StopGaming, 202
Streamlabs, 160, 161, 163
Sun-Higginson, Shannon, 185–188
Supercell, 71, 83–84, 87, 88, 109
Super Mario Run, 98–101
Sussman, Clifford, 208

T
Taylor, Bev, 124
Taylor, T. L., 128, 144
Tencent, 41, 70, 71, 109
Terdiman, Daniel, 21
Travel Frog, 111–112
trolling, 9, 189–192
Trump, Donald, 196–198
Twine, 173–184
Twitch, 7, 9, 43, 67, 74, 113, 124, 134–137, 139, 140, 141, 143, 144, 148, 149, 150, 151, 152, 156, 160–164
Twitter, 45, 52, 76, 90, 125, 131, 160, 162, 166, 168, 189, 191, 192

U
Ultra Business Tycoon III, 182

V
Vesterbacka, Peter, 87, 88
Vigneault, Brian C., 148, 150

W
Wallace, Mark, 19
Whyte, Keith S., 204
Wickham, Rich, 115
women and gaming, 9, 26, 51, 61–62, 64, 66–68, 141–145, 165–169, 174, 177, 178, 185–188
Woo Jong-Sik, 116, 118
Woolley, Liz, 203–204
Words With Friends, 9, 102, 105–106, 109
World of Warcraft, 7, 24–29, 61, 69–70, 90, 151, 194, 198, 201, 206
Wu, Brianna, 168
Wyatt, Ryan, 59, 161, 163–164

Y
Yee, Nick, 17, 18
YouTube, 7, 25, 35, 43, 48, 58–60, 65, 72, 74, 113, 124, 127, 131, 139, 140, 149, 152, 153, 156, 160, 161–162, 163, 164, 170, 192

Z
Zacconi, Riccardo, 90, 91
Zennstrom, Niklas, 88
Zynga, 75–82, 91, 107, 109

This book is current up until the time of printing. For the most up-to-date reporting, visit www.nytimes.com.